THE
LONG
ITALIAN
LUNCH

Julie Biuso

photography by
Ian Batchelor

RANDOM
HOUSE
NEW ZEALAND LTD

A RANDOM HOUSE BOOK
Published by Random House New Zealand
18 Poland Road, Glenfield, Auckland, New Zealand

First published 1998

ISBN 1 86941 347 4

Design: Juliet Hughes
Cover photograph: Ian Batchelor
Printed in Hong Kong

CONTENTS

In memory of Mamma Rosa, and to Margot, Marcella and Isanna, with much gratitude

Non ho fatto fatica a credere che l'incontro di Julie con la famiglia Biuso abbia rappresentato per lei il momento della scintilla, dell'inappellabile e definitivo innamoramento per l'Italia. Quando ho avuto occasione di pranzare con Julie, di assaporare i piatti e l'atmosfera di casa sua ho avuto come la sensazione che un destino si fosse, per una volta, compiuto secondo copione. Julie esperta e appassionata di cucina, Julie che sa che cucinare significa preparare un piacere, Julie che ama le famiglie numerose che intorno all tavola danno il meglio di sè in fatto di chiasso, conversazioni, umorismo, Julie l'Irlandese solare, con tutti i retaggi di musica, allegria e convivialità della sua terra, incontra un Italiano, per il quale valgono esattamente gli stessi valori, le stesse regole del buon vivere, le stesse priorità. E incontra, con lui, la ricchezza, l'opulenza della cucina italiana.

Non poteva che essere amore, privato e professionale.

Credo che questo libro nasca da quella passione senza rimedio. Julie ha studiato, ha portato avanti un lavoro di ricerca assolutamente corretto e scientifico. Ma sotto tutta questa razionalità, sotto la pignoleria e l'attenzione professionale c'era un entusiasmo assoluto, allegrissimo, il desiderio di condividere un grande piacere. Secondo me il sogno di Julie è quello di invitare a pranzo una quantità esagerata di persone, e di cucinare per loro. Vorrebbe servire a questa tavolata immensa i piatti che lei ama per farli amare anche dai suoi commensali. Vorrebbe conversare con ognuno di loro, sapere se quello che stanno mangiando li entusiasma come lei si è entusiasmata nel cucinarlo; ma vorrebbe anche chiacchierare d'altro, di come è andata la giornata, e come stanno i bambini e che progetti hanno per le vacanze. Questo libro è per lei quanto di più vicino a questo sogno. Julie non può invitarvi tutti quanti a pranzo; ma gli splendidi piatti che vorrebbe cucinare per voi ve li offre su queste pagine. Leggete e provate a realizzarli: siete suoi ospiti.

CARLO PETRINI, SLOW FOOD MOVEMENT

It wasn't hard for me to see that Julie's encounter with the Biuso family was the spark that ignited her lasting love for Italy. When I had the opportunity to dine with Julie, to savour the dishes and the atmosphere of her home, I got the feeling that for once, destiny was unfolding according to an imaginary script. Julie the passionate cook; Julie who knows that to cook is to give pleasure; Julie who loves big families crowded around the table, chatting and laughing uproariously; Julie with her sunny Irish heritage of music, joy and conviviality, meets an Italian who has the same values, the same love of the good life. With him she discovers the riches, the opulence of Italian cuisine.

It couldn't have been anything else but love, private and professional.

I believe this book is born from that inevitable passion. Julie has carefully researched *The Long Italian Lunch;* but beneath the attention to detail, there is an irrepressible, joyful enthusiasm — the desire to share a great pleasure. It seems to me that Julie's dream is to invite to lunch an enormous number of people, and to cook for them. She would serve at this banquet the dishes she loves, so that her guests can love them too. She would talk to each of them, to find out if what they are eating is delighting them in the same way it delighted her to prepare it. But she would also chat about other things . . . how their day was going, how their children were, what plans they had for the holidays . . .

This book is for her the closest thing to her dream. Julie cannot invite every one of you to lunch, but the splendid dishes that she would cook for you are offered on these pages. Read and try to recreate them. You are her guests.

TRANSLATED BY REMO BIUSO

I t seems as if the whole of Italy grinds to a halt daily at 1.00 pm. You can just about hear the dinner gong reverberating through the land. It's lunchtime, feast-time, family-time, time to replenish, time to nourish body and soul, time to relax. Eat to your heart's content, wash it down with copious draughts of red wine, argue with the wife, husband, kids, or in-laws, play raucous games with the over-indulged children and bounce the baby or grandchild on the knee. Then a snooze on the couch or in bed — alone, or with your partner if you're feeling frisky.

By 3.30 pm, shadows creep behind drawn shutters. Hushed houses slowly come back to life. Bus drivers stir from their siestas, wash the sleep from their eyes, and start up the buses again. The long lunch is over for another day. Body and soul rejuvenated, it's back to work till seven; plenty of time to digest, and make use of, the food consumed.

On high days and holidays, meals are more lavish and leisurely. Work is not on the agenda, but perhaps soccer is — either on the television, or a live game. Otherwise, there is the Sunday promenade. Don the best clothes and shoes, coiffe the hair, adorn the body with bangles and baubles, apply a gash of lipstick — then out onto the streets to strut. Everyone looks grand. The children are spoiled rotten, with icecreams, sweets, balloons. The pigeons are fed, chased and terrorised to within an inch of their lives. Then the chill evening air drives everyone back into the warmth of their homes — to the kitchen, the heart of the house. But in summertime, life on the streets continues until the houses have cooled down and being inside becomes tolerable again.

Baked Croissants
with Sugared Fruit

I love long Italian lunches. From the moment I sat at a crowded table, jostling elbows with laughing, cajoling, arguing Italians, I was smitten. Like any newcomer to the Italian table, I ate like there was no tomorrow. But I quickly learned I was no match for the Italians. They had been in training since birth, and loading up on button-popping carbohydrates in short takes was second nature to them. Coming from the land of meat and three veg, I had to seriously reorganise my stomach to keep pace. I never really caught up, and many's the time I felt in need of a crane to lift me off my chair

I'm a family person, of Irish descent somewhere along the line, the youngest of ten children. I grew up at a crowded, noisy table. From the very first, Italy felt comfortable to me. The Irish and the Italians are similar in many ways: family — big families — revelry, music and song. They love to talk, gossip and debate. Fun and pleasure are high on the agenda.

I swapped my Irish name for an Italian one twenty years ago without a trace of guilt. It is easy for me these days to feel Italian. Still, I'm afraid to go to Ireland because I may never leave. And that's where I'm at today — somewhere between Irish and Italian, with my New Zealand upbringing meshing the two together.

But back to the long Italian lunch. These days everyone seems to be on a treadmill — the faster things get done, the better. I believe it's at the expense of pleasure. In a typical Italian–Irish way I ask, how can you enjoy anything if it's over so fast?

I remember standing on a street corner in New York when I was sixteen, watching the parade of life spin by. People were power-walking, long before it was fashionable, and many were actually running. It was frightening. Everyone was in a frenzy to get somewhere. Nearly thirty years later, the rest of the world has caught up and has bought into that frenzied pace. Fast food is getting faster — it has to be ready NOW. And foodwriters are constantly telling people, 'No one wants to spend long in the kitchen these days.'

Nothing makes me madder. We are scaring people out of the kitchen, making them feel guilty about time spent lovingly preparing food. Soon our young won't know how to cook — only how to reheat and serve ready-made food. Well, I want to make a stand. I'm all for the family, warts and all, coming together at mealtimes, gathering around the table, eating together, discussing, sharing, debating, arguing, yahooing. Not that I am averse to good planning and sensible shortcuts; you'll find many tips throughout the book which help save time at no expense to the finished dish. But I want for people, just occasionally, to *slow down*, spend a bit of time in the kitchen making something delicious, something which will bring joy to family and friends, and enrich their lives.

That's what is inside my heart. I've always loved cooking because it's a way of giving pleasure to people, while strengthening bonds with family and friends. Enjoy then, the time it takes to make and eat these Long Italian Lunches.

THE STORIES

My intention with this book was to show Italy as I've experienced it — the good times and the bad. If most of the tales have a positive edge, it's because Italy's like that.

I visited Italy 'incognito', not as a journalist, and I was treated no differently to anyone else. My privilege has been to be invited into the Biuso family and immersed in their love.

If you know Italy, and the Italians, I hope you will find some humour in my observations. If you've never been there, I hope *The Long Italian Lunch* inspires you to go.

NOTES ON THE MENUS

Of course these menus don't have to be served at noon. A two o'clock start might suit you better, or three o'clock, or four — there are no rules.

In all cases, I suggest doing advance preparation the day before. Most of the menus take two to three hours of preparation on the day, and you would be hard pressed to do everything — as well as the shopping, and serving the food — in a morning. And depending on the kind of atmosphere you want to create, you could ask some of your guests to come early and give you a hand.

Don't hurry the food. Make sure people have plenty of time, with breaks between courses. And plenty of wine, plenty of water, plenty of fun and laughter.

Firstly, I wish to thank Juliet Rogers, Harriet Allan and Michael Moynahan from Random House for deciding to run with this project. Harriet has been a guiding light through the lengthy period of writing and producing this book, aided by senior editor Gillian Kootstra, who juggled the difficult job of editing the copy without changing my style. Thanks also to Juliet Hughes for the clever and uncluttered design.

Ray Richards, my literary agent, deserves a very big thank you for putting me in touch with Random, and for his guidance throughout.

Thanks also to Mario Magaraggia, the Italian Consular Representative in Auckland, Dr Provenzano, the Italian Ambassador in Wellington, and Carlo Petrini, Editor-in-Chief of the International Slow Food Movement; and to Claudia Roden, internationally acclaimed food writer, Antonia Allegra, past president International Association of Culinary Professionals, and Margaret Fulton, doyenne of the Australian culinary scene.

The stories and recipes have been brought to life by the wonderful photographs taken by Ian Batchelor, who possesses a great mix of professionalism, talent and wit, the last being the essential element to help us through long and late shoots; and Julie Dalzell, editor of the award-winning New Zealand magazine *Cuisine*, has given me stacks of encouragement over the eleven years I have contributed to the magazine.

Millys Kitchen Shop, Linens and More, and Country Road have all been fabulous about lending props for photographs.

Joyce Lowyim at IE Produce is a real gem. If it were possible to procure a particular vegetable or fruit that I wanted, she did it. Brian Taylor at the Meatkeeper has supplied me for years with excellent meat. Selected cheeses came from Kapiti Cheeses. Quality Italian goods came from Sabato, and Glengarry Hancocks provided wine to match the dishes in the photographs.

These thanks would not be complete without a nod to Remo, Luca and Ilaria — after all they're the ones who put up with me when I was tired and short-tempered after writing into the wee hours.

But the big thank you for this book goes to the Biuso family at large, for plying me with so much delicious food over the years that I was compelled to write about it.

JULIE BIUSO
Auckland
June 1998

High Days and Holidays

Liguria Stole My Heart

I sailed into the port of Genova (Genoa) for the first time on an ocean-going liner in 1975. From the sea, the city of Genova twinkled in the sun, beckoning me to her. Majestic buildings and crumbling palaces from a bygone era stood alongside the terracotta and ochre buildings hung with faded green shutters and festooned with potted geraniums. The apartments and houses nestled together on soft hills washed by the Ligurian sea. It was irresistible. I fell in love with Italy before I set foot on her soil.

I found myself in Genova again in 1976, running a small restaurant for the Scottish church in an old rundown three-storey building. The restaurant was part of a club intended as a home away from home for visiting Scottish sailors, but much to our relief, the club was rarely visited by sailors. Instead, it became a bustling nucleus for English-speaking foreigners, both permanent residents and travellers passing through, and for local Italians wanting to practise their halting English with the 'Inglesh gels'. It was a pretty dynamic place.

This is where I met Remo, my Italian husband. Back then he spoke just a 'lettel Inglesh' and I spoke just *un pochino d'Italiano*, but it didn't seem to matter. The rest of our communication was carried out with lots of arm-waving and raising and lowering of eyebrows. When there was any doubt, we just looked into each other's eyes and melted. It didn't seem to matter.

I first met Mamma Rosa, Remo's mother, by chance on the street. She immediately invited me for Sunday lunch. The family was dying to meet me, Remo's foreign girlfriend, the cause of his absenteeism from family meals. I didn't need a second invitation, I went willingly. On entering the portals of their spacious and gracious home, my life was to change forever. Although I didn't realise it at the time, Italy, for better or worse, was seeping into my soul and soon there would be no going back, no going without her anymore.

The Biuso family at that time consisted of Mamma Rosa and Papà Michele, Remo's father, Mamma Rosa's brother, Zio Pasqualino, Remo's eldest sister Margot and her two children, Annamaria and Eugenio, and his second sister Marcella and her husband Alberto. But the numbers swelled at weekends, on saints' days and for celebratory events. There were often twenty at the table, twice a day, with Remo's brother Ferruccio, his wife Isanna and their two children Corrado and Valeria.

Poussins with Crunchy Prosciutto and Sage Butter

I loved being in the kitchen when Mamma Rosa was preparing food. My favourite perch was by the window with a view over the Castello d'Albertis. It was the one window in the house which looked out over lots of greenery and it was often flooded with sunlight. I was never asked to help then. I was treated like a guest for ages and given the second most important seat at the table, next to Zio, one seat down from Papà. I never actually worked out how I lost my dinner-table ranking, but over the years I slowly slid down the table until I came to my resting place, at the opposite end of the table next to Marcella and across from Alberto. I knew by then that I was as much a part of the family as any other member.

Mamma Rosa

The cooking in Mamma Rosa's kitchen was an intriguing mix of Genovese dishes with influences from Tuscany, Sicily and Emilia-Romagna. When I first met her Mamma Rosa was sixty-two years old and showed no signs of handing over the reins. A skilled cook, among other things she had mastered the frying pan better than anyone I know. Her food always emerged crackling crisp and golden, never heavy or greasy. She wasn't afraid of heat or spluttering oil — her cooking clothes, the kitchen walls and floor were testament to that — and that was her secret in producing perfectly fried foods.

I loved watching her elegant hands, with the pointy well-kept nails, preparing food. She'd disappear into the cellar and return with an armful of garlic, onions and potatoes and set about peeling and chopping. Like me, she rarely cut herself, even though the knives were often blunt, though, also like me, she would burn herself often.

She would lift up one of the heavy wooden chopping boards, impregnated with garlic, which had been set to dry by the side of the oven after the previous meal and take down the *mezzaluna*, a chopper shaped like a half moon, from the dish-draining cupboard above the sink. Then she would begin. Whole garlic cloves would be put on the board and chopped to a near paste with the rhythmic to-ing and fro-ing of the mezzaluna blade. She always looked at peace doing this. She had mastered the rhythm of the mezzaluna long ago, not too slow or it would take forever, not too fast or the garlic would fly off the board. Strong arms, plenty of muscle, keeping it at a steady pace.

The garlic, along with the onion, would be melted in olive oil in an old black pan, then cubed potatoes would be added and cooked to a crisp. The mixture was transferred to a bowl, a handful of grated crumbs thrown in, some seasoning and herbs too, then lastly some eggs. This was how she made her potato frittata. The ingredients were stirred, returned to a hot well-oiled pan and cooked till lacy and crisp. It was unbelievably good. Whenever we took one of Mamma Rosa's farewell frittata snacks, a great golden wedge of sautéd potatoes and onion, suspended in crispy parmesan and egg, reeking of garlic, dripping in delicious olive oil, and stuffed into slices of crusty country bread, and ate them on trains and boats, people next to us sniffed the air and looked at us longingly. It was obvious that what we were eating was delicious. Ah, Mamma Rosa, you were a damn good cook!

The recipe for her exquisite potato frittata is on page 97. You're mad if you don't try it.

When I think back to the thin buckled pans she cooked in, the wooden chopping boards warped through excessive use of the mezzaluna, the lack of space and equipment, the mouths to feed, twice a day, day after day, I have nothing but admiration for her.

Her food was an enticement to come and visit, to stay, to linger longer than intended. Most of my Italian cooking skills have been learned in her kitchen, with her and her daughters and daughter-in-law.

What else was special about Mamma Rosa? Her voice, her beautiful melodic voice. She loved to sing opera and old folk songs when she cooked, when she washed and when she ironed. Her voice was soft, and when she sang I wanted the rest of the world to be quiet so I could listen more intently. I knew she was happy when she sang. Her daughter Margot also sings beautifully, with a husky, haunting quality.

We have a wonderful painting of a farm scene on our walls painted by Mamma Rosa when she was thirteen. She could have been a serious artist, though there was no possibility of that in her lifetime. She was raised a good Catholic girl; she had a family, not a career. Still, she painted throughout her life, on scraps of cloth and silk, anything she could lay her hands on. All the family members have framed works in their homes. It's with some regret, we feel, that she didn't personally see the abstract paintings her grandson, our son, Luca, painted before he turned eight. She would have been so proud to see that the skill and the tradition have flowed to another generation.

We remember her food, her art, her singing, her prayers. She was a great believer in prayer. She prayed for all mankind. She prayed especially hard for her loved ones. She prayed for me to have healthy, happy children.

Since I have been part of the Biuso family there have been plenty of births, christenings and marriages celebrated around the long dining table in the family home. There have been times of sadness too, as there are in all families. The most significant events are recorded in various tales throughout this book.

Papà died in December 1994 and Mamma in November 1996; but hey, they didn't do too badly — Papà was eighty-five and Mamma was eighty-two. They left behind a wealth of wonderful memories for their children and grandchildren to remember them by, including me, the 'foreigner' they welcomed into the family.

HIGH DAYS AND HOLIDAYS

SERVES 6

SUMMER MENU

Strawberry Prosecco

Seared Scallops with Caper and Fennel Dressing
or
Shellfish Risotto

Poussins with Crunchy Prosciutto and Sage Butter
Crispy Risotto Cakes (or a green salad)
Baby Peas and Shallots

Late Summer Fruit Salad

WINTER MENU

Mamma Rosa's Arancini
or
Polenta Toasties with Creamy Mushroom Sauce

Baked Nut of Veal with Marsala Glaze
Withered Carrots
Stewed Leeks

Panettone Pudding

Strawberry Prosecco

MENU NOTES

I associate Italian holidays and festivals with summer. It's hot. The windows are pulled open first thing in the morning to let in the cooler morning air, then shuttered to repel the heat as soon as it starts to penetrate the buildings. Even so, there is scarcely a breath of air. The kitchen is stifling. But no one complains too much. We all dream of cooling off in the sea. Water means fish and shellfish — an obvious starter for a meal.

The quick way with scallops in SEARED SCALLOPS WITH CAPER AND FENNEL DRESSING ensures they stay plump and juicy while retaining their fresh sea flavours, which are enhanced by the salty tang of capers. I've taken a bit of licence with this recipe and added the red capsicum accompaniment; I like the contrast of salty tang against its sweetness.

The seafood theme is continued with a SHELLFISH RISOTTO. Try this some time as a main course for four — it's particularly good as a light summer lunch consumed outdoors in a shady spot, or as an early evening summer starter followed by a simple grilled fish. If you're doing the whole menu, the risotto will serve 6, but you will need to replace the Crispy Risotto Cakes with another vegetable or salad. I would opt for an interesting green leaf salad. Don't serve parmesan cheese with it (it is out of place with seafood).

The highlight of the menu is the main course of POUSSINS. They are simply gobsmackingly good. The prosciutto on top cooks to a golden crisp and the aromas of fennel, garlic and sage tease the nostrils as they cook. The poussins, wrapped in their seasoned jackets, stay moist and become fork-tender. I know they are expensive, but this is a special festive menu. I suppose, at a pinch, you could treat chicken breasts the same way (cook them for a shorter time) and although I don't recommend it, bacon could be substituted for the prosciutto. (If it's good bacon, finely sliced, it'll work well, but if it's the usual supermarket stuff pumped full of water, it'll be a disappointment.)

The RISOTTO CAKES are hugely popular. They taste buttery and nutty and everyone will be fighting over 'seconds'. I recommend frying them in clarified butter because it can maintain a higher temperature for a longer period than ordinary butter, without burning.

A real bonus about these two dishes is that they can be prepared a day ahead. All you need do on the day is bring the poussins to room temperature before cooking them — then in the oven they go, requiring one baste only during cooking. Dead easy. The risotto cakes do need last-minute frying, but they are quite well behaved in the pan and don't spit too much. They can be fried once the poussins are cooked and resting.

I've given instructions for using frozen peas if fresh peas are not available. They work well in this recipe — just ensure you use baby frozen peas.

If it's a wintry family celebration, you'll need different food. Deep-fried rice croquettes are called *ARANCINI* in Sicily, because they look like big oranges (Sicily is home to superb citrus crops). In Lazio, they're known as *supplì al telefono*, because when they're split in half, they look like a telephone receiver, with the stretched melted mozzarella looking like a telephone cord. Whatever you call them, they make superb eating, and are always a talking point. Try them some other time for a light meal, followed by salad (Italians eat them as a first 'plate' in place of pasta). If you're vegetarian, omit the Bolognese sauce. Mamma Rosa made arancini often in cooler weather, serving them mounded up in a large, deep, white china bowl, like a bowl of oranges. The bowl was old and crazed, but she couldn't part with it, and the arancini didn't look right served in anything else. Arancini should be eaten in pasta bowls, broken open with a fork and eaten like a risotto.

POLENTA TOASTIES are an alternative. You can shortcut the preparation with instant polenta, which cooks in about 5 minutes. If using regular polenta, check if it is cooked using the 'wooden spoon' test. Insert a wooden spoon in the centre of the pot. As the polenta cooks and firms, it will support the spoon. When the spoon stays upright in the middle of the polenta, and dances with the bubbling mixture, it is cooked.

If young VEAL is not an option for the main course, either because it is too expensive or not available, regular 'butcher's veal' can be used (it's not true veal because the animals have usually grazed outside and are more mature than the young calves used to provide veal). Lower the cooking temperature to 160°C and allow approximately 40 minutes more cooking time. Take care when using arrowroot. Yes, it's a fabulous and fast thickener, useful when you don't know the amount of liquid to thicken, which doesn't make the juices cloudy or dull — but be aware: unlike cornflour, which continues to thicken the more it is cooked, continued boiling breaks down the thickening properties of arrowroot and the sauce will become thin again. Also, remember, a little is better than a lot.

The CARROTS are another winner. Sliced then simmered in water and butter till tender and finished with parmesan cheese, their savoury flavours go with many dishes. Don't be tempted to serve them crunchy — you'll be missing the point. They should be cooked till tender, in reducing amounts of buttery water which intensifies their sweetness. Just make sure they don't fry.

When choosing LEEKS, look for young slim ones, then you will be able to cook them whole in the pan as described. If these cannot be found, use regular leeks, but cut them in half down the length then into fat slices and cook until tender. These leeks work with most meat dishes, but are particularly good with veal and chicken. The Marchese de Frescobaldi (head of the Frescobaldi Wine Estate in Tuscany) once ate at my table. I served him these leeks with the veal and Marsala glaze which he greatly appreciated as, apparently, he is never served leeks at home.

In Italy you might collect a dessert or a selection of pastries from the local *pasticceria* for a celebratory meal, but I've taken a more homespun approach and provided sweet finishings for both menus. The SUMMER FRUIT SALAD of plump apricots and strawberries is an extraordinary combination, and gives a light finish to the rich meal.

Come winter time, a pudding with more substance will be welcome. This one made with almonds and dried apricots and PANETTONE (a raised sweet bread popular at Christmas-time) layered with a light custard, is a sort of Italian version of bread and butter pud and seems to keep everyone content. I often make it with the soft crumbs scooped out of *brioche* that I have used for another dish. (I brush the brioche with melted butter, flavoured sometimes with garlic, bake them until crisp and fill with a savoury or sweet filling.) I keep the crumbs in a bag in the freezer until I have enough to turn into a dessert (there's nothing to beat Italian frugality!). Remember with this dessert that you need to soak the apricots ahead. Rinse the vanilla pod well, dry it and store it till next time, or put it in a jar of castor sugar, to which it will impart a wonderful vanilla flavour.

The STRAWBERRY PROSECCO is such a fun festive drink, I hope you'll try it (it works fine with cheaper bubblies too). Although the summer menu calls for strawberries twice, they come at each end of the menu and are in different forms, so it won't seem repetitive.

STRAWBERRY PROSECCO

per drink allow:
³/₄ cup hulled strawberries
¹/₂ teaspoon lemon juice
and ¹/₄ teaspoon castor sugar
1–2 bottles Prosecco (a sparkling dry Italian wine)

Purée the strawberries in a food processor or liquidiser then push through a sieve. Transfer the purée to a glass jug and stir in the lemon juice and sugar. The purée can be prepared 30 minutes before serving.

Just before serving, pour in an equal quantity of chilled Prosecco. Stir. When the foam subsides, pour carefully into champagne flutes. Serve immediately.

SEARED SCALLOPS WITH CAPER AND FENNEL DRESSING

SERVES 6

600 g scallops, rinsed and patted dry
1–2 tablespoons olive oil
2 tablespoons capers, chopped
60 ml (4 tablespoons) extra virgin olive oil
¹/₄ teaspoon salt
freshly ground black pepper to taste
15 ml (1 tablespoon) lemon juice
2 tablespoons chopped fennel leaves
half a large red capsicum, finely diced

Put the scallops in a bowl and drizzle over olive oil. Toss them gently in the bowl until they are coated in oil. Heat a large heavy-based frying pan over a medium-high heat. When the pan is hot, put in some of the scallops (don't crowd the pan — cook in two or three batches) and cook them on both sides for a few minutes until nearly cooked through. Transfer to a bowl as they are done.

Mix the capers, 3 tablespoons of extra virgin olive oil, salt, pepper, lemon juice and one tablespoon of chopped fennel together in a small bowl.

Heat the diced red capsicum in a pan with 1 tablespoon of extra virgin olive oil and a little black pepper, and cook gently until tender. When all the scallops are cooked, pour over the dressing and pile onto a serving plate. Garnish with diced capsicum, sprinkle over the remaining fennel and serve immediately.

Seared Scallops with Caper and Fennel Dressing

Shellfish Risotto

Serves 6

400 g prepared squid tubes
100 ml extra virgin olive oil
1 small onion, finely chopped
2 cloves garlic, crushed
3 tablespoons finely chopped parsley
400 g can Italian tomatoes, drained then mashed
200 g shrimps
12 mussels
12 cockles
250 ml dry white wine
400 g (about 1³/₄ cups) Italian risotto rice
(arborio, vialone nano, carnaroli)
salt

Wash the squid and remove any loose matter and any plastic-like 'beaks'. Chop the flesh roughly, then process it until finely chopped but not paste-like (alternatively chop finely by hand). Put 75 ml of the olive oil in a heavy-based saucepan and add the onion. Cook over a low heat until the onion is translucent then add the garlic. When it is pale golden add 2 tablespoons of the parsley, stir it around then add the squid. Cook for 2–3 minutes, until the squid turns dull white, then tip in the tomatoes, cover the pan and cook gently for 30 minutes, stirring occasionally.

Rinse the shrimps and remove any darkish veins; drain. Scrub the mussels and remove beards as described on page 113. Clean and soak the cockles. Clean the mussels in a frypan with the wine, cover and set over a high heat. Cook until the mussels open, then using tongs, transfer them to a side plate. Next, put the cockles in the frypan and repeat the process. Line a small sieve with kitchen paper and set it over a bowl. Pour on the wine juices and strain. Remove the mussels from their shells and check that all the beard is removed. Remove the cockles from their shells and add them to the mussels and cover.

In a separate pan bring 2 litres of water to a simmer. Add the rice to the tomato and squid mixture and stir well to coat the grains. Sauté for 2 minutes, stirring often with a wooden spoon, then stir in a ladleful of hot water. This will evaporate quickly. Add a second ladleful of hot water and stir gently but continuously until the liquid has nearly evaporated. Continue cooking in this way, stirring continuously (if you don't stir, the rice will stick), adding more water once the rice starts to dry out, for about 20 minutes. Then incorporate the strained wine liquor and continue cooking until the rice is just tender. Quickly stir through the mussels, cockles and shrimps. Heat through for 1–2 minutes, then blend in a few pinches of salt, the remaining olive oil and 1 tablespoon of parsley. Serve immediately.

SERVES 6

6 poussins
70 g butter, melted
$1/2$ teaspoon salt
freshly ground black pepper to taste
$1^1/2$ teaspoons fennel seeds
4 cloves garlic, crushed
$1^1/2$ tablespoons chopped sage leaves
300 g thinly sliced prosciutto
50 ml dry white wine
herbs for garnishing (small clumps of sage, rosemary and parsley)

Rinse the poussins inside and out, removing necks, etc, from cavities. Pat dry. Mix the butter, salt, pepper, fennel seeds, garlic and sage together in a small bowl. Put half a teaspoon of the mixture inside each poussin. Fold the wing tips back then tie the legs and parson's nose together with string on each poussin.

Brush the poussins generously with the seasoned butter then wrap prosciutto around them (put more on the top than on the underside). Put the poussins in a large roasting dish (there should be space around each poussin so they brown and don't stew) and transfer to an oven preheated to 190°C. Cook 35–50 minutes (this depends on the size of the poussins; check juices are clear by piercing a thigh with a skewer, or partially separate one leg from the body of one of the poussins and check that the flesh is cooked).

Brush the poussins with more of the seasoned butter 15 minutes before cooking time is up, and again when you take them from the oven. Let them rest for 15 minutes, loosely draped with a piece of aluminium foil, then transfer them to a board and snip off the string.

Pour off any fat from the roasting dish and set the dish over a medium heat and pour in the wine. Bubble up, then distribute the juices between six hot dinner plates. Put a poussin on each plate, garnish with herbs and serve immediately with the risotto cakes and baby peas and onion. If preferred, the poussins can be arranged sitting on top of the risotto cakes.

CRISPY RISOTTO CAKES

SERVES 6

1.2 litres chicken stock
30 ml (2 tablespoons) olive oil
50 g butter
1 small onion, finely chopped
1 clove garlic, crushed
125 ml dry white wine
400 g (about 2 cups) Italian rice (arborio, vialone nano, carnaroli)
¼ teaspoon salt
freshly ground black pepper to taste
freshly grated nutmeg
50 g (½ cup) freshly grated parmesan cheese
3 eggs, beaten well together in a small bowl
clarified butter (as required)

Bring the chicken stock to simmering point in a saucepan, then set the heat so that it is kept very hot, but does not boil and evaporate.

Choose a 2.5–3 litre heavy-based saucepan. Set it over a medium heat, put in the olive oil and half the butter and add the onion and garlic. Sauté until a pale golden colour, then pour in the wine and cook until it has nearly evaporated.

Tip in the unwashed rice, sauté for 2 minutes, stirring often with a wooden spoon, then stir in a ladleful of hot stock. This will evaporate quickly. Add a second ladleful of stock and stir gently, but continuously, until the stock has evaporated. Continue cooking in this way, stirring every few seconds (if you don't stir, the rice will stick), adding more stock once the rice is no longer soupy. It is ready when, like pasta, the grains are al dente. Aim to finish with the risotto dryer than is usual for a finished risotto (it should be threatening to stick on the bottom of the pan).

Remove the pan from the heat, add salt, black pepper, nutmeg, the rest of the butter and the parmesan cheese. Beat well for 1 minute, cover with a lid and leave to cool for 30 minutes, then beat in enough egg to make the mixture tacky but not sloppy. Refrigerate until firm (the risotto mixture can be be prepared a day in advance).

When ready to cook the risotto cakes, roll the rice into approximately ten large balls, then flatten these slightly into plump discs (serve extra cakes separately).

Heat a large heavy-based frying pan and drop in 2 knobs of clarified butter. Carefully lower in the first batch of risotto cakes. Cook over a medium heat until golden and crisp then turn them carefully and cook the second side, flattening them slightly with a spatula. Transfer to a plate lined with crumpled kitchen paper and repeat the process with the rest of the risotto cakes. Serve hot with the poussins and peas.

Poussins with Crunchy Prosciutto and Sage Butter served
on Crispy Risotto Cakes with Baby Peas and Shallots

Baby Peas and Shallots

Serves 6

knob of butter
200 g shallots, peeled and separated
1¹/₂ tablespoons flour
1 cup water
generous 1 kg fresh peas (should yield more than 3 cups shelled peas),
or 500 g frozen baby peas
¹/₄ teaspoon salt
freshly ground black pepper to taste

Set a heavy-based saucepan over a low to medium heat and drop in the butter. When it has melted, add the shallots and cook gently until well browned. Stir in the flour then pour in the water and bring to the boil (if need be, you can prepare the recipe a few hours ahead up to this point). Add the peas, salt and pepper.

Return the liquid to the boil, cover with a lid and cook 15–20 minutes, or until the peas are tender, on a very low heat.

If a lot of liquid accumulates during cooking, lift off the lid and cook quickly until it evaporates. Serve immediately.

If using frozen peas, tip them into a sieve and rinse with hot tap water until the ice crystals melt. Add to the pan, bring to the boil, then cook very gently for 10 minutes as described.

Late Summer Fruit Salad

Serves 6

grated rind and juice of 1 lemon
juice of 1 orange
1 tablespoon castor sugar
1 punnet strawberries
500 g plump, just-ripe apricots, washed
fresh mint leaves

Put the lemon rind and the citrus juices into a bowl. Stir in the sugar. Hull the strawberries, slice each berry into 2–3 pieces and add to the bowl. Slice the apricots into smallish wedges and add to the strawberries. Toss well, ensuring all the fruit is covered with juice. Cover and chill for 2–3 hours (the fruit can be prepared several hours ahead if necessary). Tear the mint leaves into small pieces and scatter over the fruit.

MAMMA ROSA'S ARANCINI

MAKES 6 (or 12 smaller ones)

2 tablespoons butter
300 g (about 1^1/$_2$ cups) Italian rice (arborio, vialone nano, carnaroli)
800–900 ml light stock
freshly ground black pepper to taste
^{1}/$_4$ teaspoon salt
50 g (^{1}/$_2$ cup) freshly grated parmesan cheese
1 egg yolk
1 small ball (25 g) fresh bocconcini mozzarella in whey,
drained on kitchen paper and cut into 12 cubes
^{1}/$_4$ cup frozen baby peas, blanched and drained (optional)
^{1}/$_4$ cup ragù sauce, homemade tomato sauce or Isanna's Porcini Ragù (page 150)
1 egg, lightly beaten
50 g (^{1}/$_2$ cup) fine, dry breadcrumbs, preferably homemade (if making
12 small balls, you will need more crumbs)
oil for deep frying

Melt the butter in a medium-sized saucepan over a high heat. Add the rice and cook for 2–3 minutes, stirring, until it smells nutty.

Meanwhile, bring the stock to the boil in a separate saucepan, then add it to the rice, a little at a time, as described in SHELLFISH RISOTTO on page 20. Cook for 15 minutes in total, then stir gently until dryish. Add plenty of pepper, salt and the parmesan cheese. Tip the rice out onto a clean board or tray (a Swiss roll tin is ideal) and spread it flat with a knife. Leave until cool.

Put the rice in a bowl and blend in the egg yolk. Spread 1–2 tablespoons of the rice in the cupped palm of one hand, put in a piece of mozzarella, a few peas and a small dollop of sauce, then another piece of mozzarella. Cover with 1–2 tablespoons rice, then carefully mould into a ball, squeezing gently, keeping the filling in the centre (this is sticky work, but easy enough to do).

When all the arancini are rolled, pass each one through the beaten egg and coat with breadcrumbs. The arancini can be prepared an hour or two in advance; keep them at room temperature.

Heat the oil to 180°C in a deep-fryer, then lower in the arancini (best done in two batches). Cook them for several minutes until they are an even, rich golden-brown (turn them in the oil once or twice to ensure they brown evenly). Lift them out with a slotted spoon and drain briefly on kitchen paper. Serve hottish (or warm — in fact they're not bad cold on a picnic), with extra sauce, if liked.

Serves 6

1.25 ml water
250 g coarse polenta
salt
1 tablespoon butter
300 g button mushrooms, thickly sliced
2 large cloves garlic, crushed
¹/₂ cup cream
freshly ground black pepper to taste
2 tablespoons chopped Italian parsley

Make the polenta first (it can be made up to two days before finishing off in the recipe; cover with plastic food wrap and refrigerate).

Bring the water to the boil in a wide, not tall and narrow, saucepan. Put the polenta in a bowl. Add 1 teaspoon of salt to the water then sprinkle on the polenta a handful at a time letting it fall through your fingers from a height. Stir continuously, using a wooden spoon. If you add the polenta too fast, it will form lumps (if this happens, fish them out because they will not break down during cooking). Once all the polenta is added, turn the heat to low and cook, giving 3–4 good stirs every 20 seconds or so, for about 25 minutes. (Check on the 'wooden spoon test' in the Menu Notes.)

Tip it out onto a wet tray and spread out about 1–1.5 cm thick. Smooth the surface and leave it to cool. Cut it into squares and cook on a clean, lightly oiled hot plate of a preheated barbecue, on in a heavy-based oiled frying pan (cast iron is good), over a medium heat until it is browned. Dish onto serving plates and top with the mushroom sauce.

To make the mushroom sauce, melt the butter in a frying pan over a medium heat. Add the mushrooms, toss well and cook until lightly browned and tender. Add the garlic and cook a minute or two until nutty-smelling. Tip in the cream, add ¹/₄ teaspoon of salt and some black pepper and cook until thickish and creamy. Mix in the parsley and spoon immediately over the hot squares of polenta.

SERVES 6

a 'nut' of veal cut from the leg or rump, weighing about 1200 g
3 cloves garlic, finely chopped
1 tablespoon finely chopped rosemary
30 ml (2 tablespoons) olive oil
large knob of butter
$^{1}/_{4}$ cup dry Marsala
freshly ground black pepper to taste
$^{3}/_{4}$ teaspoon salt
approx 50 ml dry white wine (or light stock)
$^{1}/_{2}$ tablespoon arrowroot (or as required)

With a small sharp knife make several incisions in the meat. Stuff in a little of the chopped garlic and rosemary and tie the meat into a neat shape with string. Heat a large heavy-based casserole over a medium heat (the meat should fit snugly in the casserole), drop in the oil then the butter. Brown the meat well on all sides, turning with tongs. Add the remaining garlic and rosemary and allow the garlic to colour to a light nut brown, then pour on the Marsala. Cook 1–2 minutes, turning the meat over in the bubbling liquid, then grind over black pepper, sprinkle salt over all sides of the meat, and pour in 2 tablespoons of the wine. Cover and bake in an oven preheated to 180°C for 1 hour, basting and turning every 20 minutes; add more wine if the liquid level drops to less than 2 tablespoons.

Remove the casserole from the oven and leave it covered for 10 minutes. Transfer the meat to a board, cover loosely with aluminium foil and place the casserole back on the heat. Scoop off and discard any fat. Mix a little arrowroot with water and tip it into the juices, then bring to the boil, stirring. Taste for seasoning, adding more salt if necessary. Cover and remove from the heat.

Remove the string from the meat, carve into thin slices and arrange on a heated plate. Spoon over the Marsala glaze and serve immediately.

SERVES 6

900 g carrots
2 knobs butter (about 40 g)
$^1/_4$ teaspoon of salt
freshly ground black pepper to taste
2 tablespoons chopped Italian parsley
4 tablespoons freshly grated parmesan cheese

Peel the carrots and slice thinly. Put them in a large heavy-based frypan and dot with the butter. Pour on $^1/_2$ cup water and sprinkle on the salt.

Bring to the boil, lower the heat to medium-low and let the water evaporate. Add another $^1/_4$ cup of water (it's just enough to stop the carrots frying), and continue cooking, stirring often. Add another $^1/_4$ of water and continue cooking until it evaporates. If the carrots are not tender, add another $^1/_4$ cup of water and continue cooking, adding more water if necessary, till they are tender.

Grind on a little black pepper then transfer the carrots to a heated serving bowl. Sprinkle on the parsley and parmesan, toss and serve immediately.

If you want to make the carrots ahead, cook as described till tender then rewarm and add the parsley and parmesan just before serving.

STEWED LEEKS

SERVES 6

6–12 slim young leeks
knob of butter
$^1/_2$ cup good chicken stock
$^1/_4$ teaspoon salt
freshly ground black pepper

Trim the leeks to fit a large heavy-based frying pan. Wash them well, letting the water run inside the leaves to dislodge dirt, then put them in the frypan, dot with butter, pour in the chicken stock and season with salt and pepper. Bring to a gentle boil, partially cover with a lid and cook gently about 15 minutes, or until tender, turning the leeks once or twice.

Transfer the leeks to a heated serving dish. If there is a lot of liquid in the pan, reduce it quickly over a high heat and pour it over the leeks. Serve immediately.

PANETTONE PUDDING

SERVES 6–8

150 g (about 1 cup) dried apricots, soaked in 1¹/₂ cups water for several hours.
250 g panettone, sliced (or use sliced brioche)
butter
300 ml milk
small piece of vanilla pod
1 tablespoon castor sugar
1 egg
1 egg yolk
50 g blanched almonds, finely chopped
icing sugar

Put the apricots and juices in a small saucepan, bring to a gentle boil, then cook gently for 5 minutes, or until very tender. Drain, reserving the juices. Mash the apricots to a purée. This can be done a day in advance if wished; cover and refrigerate.

Spread most of the apricot purée over the panettone, and arrange in a buttered ovenproof dish. Spread the remaining purée over the top, along with any juices.

Put the milk, split vanilla pod and sugar into a saucepan. Heat slowly until the milk is just boiling, then set aside for 10 minutes to cool.

Beat the egg and egg yolk together in a bowl, then pour on the heated milk, stirring, to make a custard. Pour the custard around the edges of the panettone (not over the top), sprinkle on the almonds, then dot with butter.

Bake 30–40 minutes in an oven preheated to 170°C, or until most of the custard has been absorbed and the pudding is golden on top.

Remove from the oven and cool for 10 minutes. Sprinkle with icing sugar and serve. If liked, accompany the pudding with a fruit salad of autumn or winter fruits.

THE TUSCAN TABLE

Within a few short weeks of meeting Remo's family, I was invited to his sister Marcella's wedding. She was to marry Alberto Bianucci, a Tuscan man from Grosseto, a city in the south of Tuscany. The wedding was to be held in San Salvatore near Lucca, a point midway between the Biuso family home in Genova and Grosseto, where the Bianucci family lived.

We drove down to Lucca from Genova early on the morning of the wedding, along with about thirty other guests. We were greeted by a sea of faces and mild pandemonium at the house of Alberto's sister, where all the preparation was taking place. I was besieged by family and friends all eager to meet me, Remo's 'exotic' girlfriend (me?). There were hugs, kisses, handshakes and more hugs, some of which threatened to seriously restrict my breathing. One of the astonishing things about the Italians is their unrestrained, infectious warmth and friendliness. You just cannot escape it. Personal space, you know that good 30 cm you stay away from someone else's face, doesn't come into it. They are there, literally right in your face (perhaps the expression originated in Italy) — never mind the bad breath; everyone eats garlic anyway. Whether you like it or not, they'll hang onto you, cuddle you, caress your cheeks, look deeply into your eyes when you are talking, and get so close that you can smell their deodorant, or lack of it.

Essentially they are telling you they like you; and if one of theirs loves you, soon they'll love you too. You are welcome. You don't need to say anything, just smile. They'll do all the talking as they cluster around, admiring your hands, your hair, your nails, your dress, your skin, anything — for sure they'll find something nice about you — as long as you are not *cold*. It's a sin to be cold in Italy — not to respond. If you're a cold *Inglese* (which they are convinced all English speakers are) and don't respond to their good intentions, they'll feel hurt. They won't understand you one bit, and will recoil unhappily. It won't stop them trying again though, until they crack the code that makes you laugh and love and live.

I was nearly smothered by their love and good intentions that day as my personal space evaporated into a very thin veil of air. When I could take no more food, wine or adulation, I excused myself from the wedding party and joined the children playing in the courtyard. I was immediately swooped on by them, but I extracted myself with tact and escaped to walk around the vineyards. Two little bodies would not be separated from mine: eight-year-old Eugenio and nine-year-old Annamaria, Remo's sister Margot's children. They clutched my hands and as we walked along the rows of vines, I had a most amazing experience with them. We actually had a conversation. They listened to my atrocious Italian, didn't mock me, and understood every word of it, and helped me learn new words instantly. Adults seem unable to think laterally when talking to a foreigner. If a word is not exactly right they shut off; but children's minds work very quickly and search out other words which might be the right one. And so you can speak with them more easily. They were both so sweet, so polite, so quiet compared to the cacophony of the wedding festivities still ringing in my ears. I wished life could stay like that forever — innocent, gentle, loving, with the sun beating down on my back, good food and wine in my stomach, and family all around. I looked into their deep brown eyes, at their milky unblemished skins and thought them quite perfect.

They became my little helpers in Genova. They would visit me after school, watch me cook and hang around and help, dashing to the shops for me to buy something I had forgotten. One day they brought me a kitten. A stray. Would I *please* keep it? He was homeless and a bit sickly, but gorgeous and I was soon smitten. We called him Humphrey. He had grey and white fur and was a charmer. His favourite party trick was to ricochet from couch to armchair, with no regard for anyone who might be seated in either at the time: a frightening experience if he happened to surprise you just when you had nodded off in the armchair for a brief respite from all the loving, hugging and close encounters being dished out daily.

I took him to the beach once, on the train. Humphrey loved the sand. He loved the smell of the fishing boats even more. He had a ball. The Italians thought I was nuts, *pazza*. But I had to be myself and if I wanted to take a cat on a train to the beach in Italy, then that's what I would do and to hell with the stares. Anyway, having survived the wedding, which was like a massive inoculation of attention, I found I was better adjusted to the family by being different, by being myself.

Life continued. Humphrey thrived. I started learning Italian.

About Tuscany

Tuscany conjures up a kaleidoscope of images — a rich tapestry of gentle landscapes and faded blue hills straddled by vines and silvery olive trees, lit by an ethereal golden light. Castles atop hillsides, towers and monuments, stone villas built generations ago by work-

Zuccotto

worn hands, splashed with the colours of the earth — terracotta, ochre, dusty mud brown, sunset pink and olive-tree green — all scorched by the relentless summer sun and frozen in time through winter snows.

And Florence, revered city of art and culture, with its Duomo, cupola and galleries, terracotta roofs, clattering cobblestones, rust and ochre, metals forged in fire set against translucent masterpieces chiselled from cold Carrara marble. Spectacular sunsets wash over the city at day's end, softening rough edges of stone and plaster. Rich and mellow, the golden-pink haze, tinged with crimson, settles like a mantle around the city, cradling the contours, before fading into a pinky mauve twilight, then disappearing into the soft blue-grey hills on the outskirts of the city.

Then there is the mediaeval city of Siena, famous for its ancient *palio* where man pits himself against the speed of crushing horse's hooves; and Lucca, home of Tuscany's crown jewel — rich, green fragrant olive oil which shines like emeralds on plates throughout the land. But rarely will a non-Italian include in the picture-perfect fantasy of Tuscany, the Maremma, the stretch of land on the Tuscan coast in the western province of Grosseto. Outshone by sister-cities and towns, the Maremma lies in wait, ready to offer an edible cornucopia of porcupine, *porcini* and *pecorino*; wild boar, wild geese and woodcock; eels, snails, truffles and molluscs. This is no ordinary cuisine, and one the tourist often misses.

Grosseto is the southernmost provincial city of the Tuscan region, but a more interesting one is Orbetello, the city on the lagoon. Two narrow strips of land tie the small 'island' known as the Argentario to the mainland. The oldest village on the Argentario is Porto Ercole, but the island's main town is Porto Santo Stefano. Both are worth a visit. The southernmost strip of land is Tombolo di Feniglia; the other is Orbetello, a city to which I have some emotional ties, since Remo grew up here.

It was the Romans who first installed a system of eel nets in the lagoons around Orbetello. Most eels eaten throughout Italy today are bred and nurtured in these waters; they are made into soups, stuffed, soused or stewed. Look out for a regional treat — freshly caught eel rubbed with ash, threaded onto skewers with fresh bay leaf and smoked over smouldering herbs. The smoky eel kebabs are then splashed with oil and vinegar and served as a tasty tidbit, washed down with a glass of bracing white wine from Pitigliano.

Seafood is enjoyed all along the Argentario coast (the Silver Coast) and is perhaps at its best when turned into one of the many varieties of *cacciucco* (seafood soup). Soups rich with the flavours of crustaceans and molluscs, saltwater or freshwater fish, seaweeds, garlic, spicy wine and tomato reductions and olive oil. Legend has it that cacciucco should be made with five varieties of fish, one for every c in the name.

The Maremma kitchen is known above all for game. Wild boar (*cinghiale*) roasted, stewed, sauced and turned into strings of sausages, some of which are eaten raw, is on offer everywhere. Quail, woodcock, pheasant, wild goose, deer, rabbit and porcupine are enjoyed. Although porcupine is now protected, it occasionally turns up on menus. When any of the locals inadvertently run over one of the strange beasts he (it's usually a male!) will deliver it to the restaurant kitchen of some country inn. He'll later be found dining there, on porcupine for sure. The taste is sweetish and gamey, the flesh is rosy in colour and lean, with a texture like rabbit. Lamb also features often on the menus, as does *pecorino* cheese (see page 37) made from sheep's milk. In the rockier mountain areas it's more likely to be kid, which is stewed with aromatic herbs, olive oil, garlic and tomato.

You'll find it hard to avoid *girarrosto* (roasting spit) in Tuscany. Enticing aromas waft out of hotter-than-hell, hole-in-the-wall restaurants around mealtimes. The tantalising sweet smell of fat crisping on suckling kid, lamb and pork joints, chickens turning a burnished gold, bay leaves crackling in the heat as the hot fat spits onto them, and the pungent smell of oil being drawn from rosemary stalks wrapped around birds and beasts, will have you salivating in no time. The assault on your nostrils is impossible to deny and if you're hungry, there's no better place to eat than a girarrosto. The Tuscans have been cooking like this for centuries and produce juicy tender meat with crisp crackling exteriors.

Vegetarians won't be hard done by though. Grosseto is famous for its flavoursome vegetables, and soups are a great showcase for them. The simplest, *acquacotta*, which translates literally as 'cooked water', is a soup of ancient origins. In its classic form water is flavoured with onion, salt and a pinch of chilli pepper, with a little tomato if you're lucky, then poured over stale bread. Nowadays, although still essentially a simple soup, it can contain any fresh seasonal vegetables you have on hand, and it is usually enriched with eggs and finished with a sprinkling of grated pecorino. Grosseto onions are particularly prized, and if you find them on a restaurant menu, usually stuffed or baked, try them, as they are a delicious regional specialty and a fiddle to prepare at home.

There's more for vegetarians. The Tuscans are fond of beans, chickpeas, grains, and eggs, all simply prepared and cooked. A meal of *pasta e fagioli* (a soupy stew of pasta and beans) will provide you with enough substance to last a day. You might also find savoury crêpes, stuffed and rolled, in place of *cannelloni* or rolled into other shapes, smothered with grated pecorino and cooked till bubbling and crisp.

The most revered product is of course olive oil, which is used generously to flavour as well as cook food. Many Maremmani cultivate their own olives (see Irene, page 133) and take them to the local presses to be processed into thick, rich oil for their personal use.

Throw in a few snails, chestnuts, plenty of porcini and wild *ovuli* mushrooms, full-flavoured vegetables such as artichokes, fennel, capsicums, tomatoes, cardoons, yellow waxy potatoes, zucchini, asparagus, Swiss chard and green beans and herbs such as rosemary, sage, bay, basil and *nepitella* (a type of wild mint), and a huge range of fruits such as red sugar-sweet watermelon, all manner of other perfumed, juicy melons, peaches dripping sweet juice and fat squishy figs, and you can understand where some of that Tuscan pride comes from.

Even the bread is unique. The typical Tuscan loaf is an unsalted flat bread with a crisp crust and holey interior. It is particularly wheaty and creamy in flavour, and with a puddle of the new season's green peppery oil, a ripe tomato plucked from the vine and a glass of young, dry wine from Pitigliano or Scansano, you could easily believe you have found Nirvana. And that's the secret to the Maremma table, and to that of Tuscany. Dishes, older than time, perfected and perfectly made. A few carefully chosen ingredients of extraordinary quality blended together. Simple, not sophisticated. Robust, not subtle. Tuscan food, like the land's forbears, the Etruscans, is strong, sturdy and proud.

Grosseto is full of ancient historical sites, castles, towers, monuments and cave dwellings. If you are visiting the area, grab a map from the tourist office which will pinpoint the dozen or more Etruscan ruins and other places of interest. If you can visit only one historical site, make it Roselle, the Etruscan city from which Grosseto was born between the ninth and eighth centuries BC.

THE TUSCAN TABLE

SERVES 8

Eggplant and Red Capsicum Crostini

Pappardelle with Zucchini and Saffron Cream Sauce

Rabbit and Quail on the Barbecue
or
Pork Chops with Fennel and Rosemary

Irene's Fried Green Tomatoes
Cannellini Bean Purée
or
Braised Red Onions
Marcella's Potatoes

Zuccotto

A summer picnic

This menu features eggplants, capsicums, zucchini and tomatoes and is perfect for a casual, late-summer meal outdoors, where the smell of rosemary charring on the barbecue will fill the nostrils and tease the appetite.

There's nothing difficult about the EGGPLANT AND CAPSICUM CROSTINI. Fry the eggplants in a good depth of very hot oil until they turn crisp and golden (see page 84); or cook them on a barbecue; oil the slices well on both sides and cook on the hot plate. They will develop a smoky nutty flavour which is delicious. The capsicums can be done on the barbecue too.

Mountains of small firm zucchini are used in dishes such as the PAPPARDELLE PASTA throughout the summer months in Italy. The whole point of such dishes is to make the most of zucchini while they are at their peak — you'll be disappointed if you use mature watery ones which are often tinged with bitterness. Make sure you have your guests waiting at the table for the pasta; pasta dressed with a cream sauce should wait for no one. Have the serving bowl and individual bowls heated too. At some other time try this dish as a main course for six.

The simple way of cooking RABBIT, QUAIL and PORK on the barbecue produces succulent results. I have given a choice of meat courses because rabbit and quail may be hard to come by. Get the butcher to joint the rabbit for you and remove all the fat.

If you choose pork, be sure not to overcook it. There's an easy test which helps understand the degree of doneness of meat. Hold your hand in an open and relaxed state. The large thumb muscle, located between the thumb and index finger will feel very soft; this is how rare meat should feel. Stretch out the hand and the muscle will firm up. This is how medium-cooked meat should feel; this is perfect for pork. Make a clenched fist and the muscle will tighten. If you cook meat to this stage it will be well done, and some meats may be dry and difficult to cut and chew.

I have also given a choice of vegetables. The CANNELLINI BEAN, a thin long white bean with a rich creamy wheaty flavour, is favoured in Tuscany. Whipped to a dense white purée, it is sensational and even better topped with a dribble of *olio santo* (see page 114).

Rounds of FRIED GREEN TOMATOES which, if cooked correctly, are coated in a lacy crisp exterior while becoming tender and juicy inside, are the perfect accompaniment. Don't attempt the recipe with anything but green tomatoes (they can have a pale tinge of pink on them in some parts). A good tomato to use is the outdoor plum tomato which has little juice, few seeds and firm flesh. Do use an extra virgin olive oil to fry the tomatoes — the fruitiness of the oil enhances the tomato flavour — but it shouldn't be an expensive estate-bottled oil.

Does it sound too down-home for you? Fried tomatoes and white bean mash? It's typical of Tuscan cuisine — great food without frills. The cannellini beans and fried green tomatoes also make great plate-mates for well-made sausages. Some of my friends have been surprised when I've served them fried green tomatoes as part of an Italian meal, but I first ate them in Grosseto at Remo's brother-in-law's sister-in-law's place (I love these long-winded family connections). Irene serves them every summer. It's her way of dealing with the surplus of tomatoes; tomato sauce and tomato salad, exquisite though they are when made with good tomatoes, tend to pall towards the end of summer.

In case you are thinking that Irene doesn't sound very Italian, even less so than fried green tomatoes, let me put you straight. Irene is pronounced E-ray-nay and she's a

Grossetana (native of Grosseto). You can't argue with that.

Onions and potatoes are another option. RED ONIONS become translucent but retain crunch when cooked briefly in white wine and oil. Apart from the tears when peeling them (try refrigerating them for several hours beforehand), they're easy to do and can be cooked ahead and reheated at serving time.

Marcella chooses even-sized small POTATOES for her excellent way with baby spuds. She scrubs them, makes a rough slit in each and smears in a little salt, pepper and dried oregano. Then they are put in a shallow roasting dish, drizzled with extra virgin olive oil and roasted in a hot oven until tender on the inside but crisping on the skin. The whole house fills with the spicy sweet smell of oregano. It makes me salivate. At the risk of burning fingers and lips, I test one as soon as they come out of the oven. She sometimes inserts a small fresh bay leaf in each potato, and omits the oregano. It's impossible to stop eating them whichever way they are made, so always make heaps.

I often serve these potatoes as the central part of a simple family meal, with a salad made from whatever can be scratched from the garden, and perhaps some good sausages, or another vegetable dish such as the following way with capsicums. Halve them, then fill with a smattering of pinenuts and sliced garlic, drizzle with oil and roast quickly on a high temperature. Who needs to eat in a restaurant when you can whistle up treats like these?

Now, about ZUCCOTTO. This typical Florentine dessert takes its shape, or so they say, from the round dome-shaped cupola of the Duomo in Florence. There are many ways of making it — with a base of either sponge cake or boudoir biscuits, moistened with liqueur or brandy, then filled with cream, toasted nuts and chocolate. Most zuccotto I have eaten have been memorable. The version here is quite straightforward, and providing you use the right size bowl and line it with plastic food wrap you won't have any major drama in turning it out.

PECORINO

Pecorino is the name given to Italian cheeses made from ewe's milk. The second name indicates where the cheese is from, or the style in which it is made. *Pecorino Sardo* and *pecorino Siciliano* are the most pungent varieties and differ from other pecorinos because the curds are not cooked, the cheese has a higher fat content and it has a shorter ripening time. Peppercorns are added to pecorino Siciliano to make *pecorino pepato*, a pungent, spicy table cheese. *Pecorino Toscano*, eaten as a table cheese when young, has a delicate lactic taste and semi-creamy texture. It becomes more pungent, firmer and drier as it ages and it is used as a grating cheese like parmesan.

EGGPLANT AND RED CAPSICUM CROSTINI

SERVES 8

1 large eggplant
olive oil
salt
2 large red capsicums
50 g butter, softened
6 black olives, stoned and finely chopped
2 cloves garlic, crushed
1 small ciabatta loaf (or use a French baguette)
freshly ground black pepper to taste
¹/₄ cup tiny basil leaves (or chopped basil)
1 tablespoon balsamic vinegar or red wine vinegar
1 tablespoon extra virgin olive oil

Slice the eggplant and pat dry with kitchen paper.

Heat a good depth of olive oil (about half a centimetre) in a heavy-based frypan over a high heat until it is smoking. Drop in as many slices of eggplant as will fit and cook quickly on both sides until a deep golden brown. Transfer the eggplant slices to a plate lined with crumpled kitchen paper and sprinkle lightly with salt. Repeat with the rest of the eggplant.

Alternatively, barbecue the eggplant slices. The eggplant can be prepared 2–3 hours ahead to this point; keep it loosely covered with kitchen paper.

Set the capsicums on an oven rack in an oven preheated to 200°C and cook for about 20 minutes, or until blistered and charred (put a piece of aluminium foil underneath the capsicums to catch drips). Transfer to a bowl, cover with the foil or with kitchen paper, and when cool enough to handle, peel off the blackened skins and discard the cores and seeds. Chop the capsicums into strips and set aside with the juices. (The capsicums can be roasted a day before required; cover and chill.)

Mix the butter, chopped olives and garlic together in a small bowl. Slice the bread thinly, and lightly spread both sides with the olive butter (this can be done several hours head; cover with food wrap). Put the bread slices on a baking sheet in an oven preheated to 180°C and bake for about 12 minutes, or till lightly golden.

To assemble the crostini, cut the eggplant slices in half, or quarters and arrange on top of the toasted bread rounds. Mound the sliced capsicums on top. Mix a few pinches of salt into the capsicum juices along with plenty of black pepper, the basil leaves, vinegar and extra virgin olive oil. Spoon over the crostini and serve.

SERVES 6–8

75 g butter
1 large onion, finely chopped
900 g small, firm zucchini, trimmed and cut into matchsticks
freshly ground black pepper to taste
salt
$^1/_4$ teaspoon saffron strands
400 ml cream
4 egg quantity fresh pasta cut into pappardelle (4 eggs, 400 g flour,
$^3/_4$ teaspoon salt; see below)
freshly grated parmesan cheese for serving

Melt the butter in a large frypan over a low to medium heat. Add the onion and cook gently until soft, then increase the heat to medium and cook until golden. Add the zucchini, increase the heat to medium-high and cook, tossing often, about 12 minutes, or until the zucchini are tender and starting to brown. Grind over plenty of pepper and mix in half a teaspoon of salt and the saffron strands. Cook a few minutes, then pour in the cream, bring to the boil, stirring, then turn off the heat.

Meanwhile, bring a large saucepan of water to the boil, salt well, and add the pappardelle. Cook at a gentle boil, stirring gently off and on, till the pasta is al dente (2–5 minutes, depending on the dryness of the pasta). Drain the pasta, then tip it into a heated serving bowl. Pour on the hot sauce (reheat it if it has cooled down). Toss well and serve immediately with parmesan cheese.

Cutting pappardelle
Make and roll the pasta as described on page 75. Dust the pasta sheets with flour then cut into wide noodles, about 2–2.5 cm wide. Hang up to dry for an hour or so. If you like, cut the noodles with a fluted pasta cutter.

Drying pappardelle
Your neighbours might think you have strange tastes in underwear . . . but the best pasta-drying system I have come up with is a plastic-coated portable clothesline. Wipe the plastic line clean and drape the pasta over it. If you have a clothesline which is not very clean, drape waxed paper over the line first (peg it in place if necessary).

Dry the pappardelle until they start turning leathery (don't dry them totally or they will become brittle), then transfer them to a tray lined with waxed paper and leave uncovered until ready to cook them (up to 4 hours in advance). You will need to check that they don't start sticking — it depends on the humidity. If they do, rehang them.

Rabbit on the Barbecue

Serves 4–6

1 stalk of rosemary
90 ml (6 tablespoons) extra virgin olive oil
3 cloves garlic, roughly chopped
1 teaspoon dried oregano, crumbled
¹/₄ teaspoon salt
freshly ground black pepper
1 rabbit, all fat removed, and cut into joints

Remove the spikes from the rosemary and chop roughly. Mix the olive oil, garlic, oregano, rosemary, salt and pepper in a bowl. Add the rabbit joints and stir to coat in the mixture. Cover and refrigerate 2–3 hours, turning occasionally; bring to room temperature before cooking.

Cook the rabbit joints over glowing coals, turning from time to time and anointing often with the marinade. Alternatively, cook them on a barbecue grill to begin with, then once coloured, transfer them to a barbecue hot plate to finish off cooking.

They will take 35–40 minutes to cook. It is better to cook them over an even moderate heat than to cook them quickly over high heat which dries the meat. Rabbit meat contains little fat and needs to be anointed frequently with the marinade to keep it moist.

Quail on the Barbecue

Serves 6

1 stalk of rosemary
90 ml (6 tablespoons) extra virgin olive oil
3 cloves garlic, roughly chopped
1 teaspoon dried oregano, crumbled
¹/₄ teaspoon salt and freshly ground black pepper to taste
6 quail

Remove the spikes from the rosemary and chop roughly. Mix the olive oil, garlic, rosemary, oregano, salt and pepper together in a bowl.

Snip each quail through the breast and spread them flat. Rinse and pat them dry.

Layer them in a bowl, spreading marinade generously over each as you do so, then drizzle the rest of the marinade over the top.

Cover and refrigerate for several hours; bring to room temperature before cooking.

Cook the quail on a preheated barbecue hot plate, skin side down, for about 12 minutes, then turn and cook the second side for about 12 minutes. Finish off over the grill rack, letting the flames lick and singe the quail for 1–2 minutes. Transfer to a plate and serve warmish.

Pork Chops with Fennel and Rosemary

Serves 8

1 stalk of rosemary
90 ml (6 tablespoons) extra virgin olive oil
1½ teaspoons fennel seeds
16 fresh bay leaves
freshly ground black pepper
8 large cloves garlic, chopped
8 large pork chops or cutlets
salt

Remove the spikes from the rosemary, chop roughly and put in a large shallow container with the olive oil, fennel seeds, bay leaves, black pepper and garlic. Mix together with a fork then put in the chops or cutlets. Spread the mixture over the meat, cover with plastic wrap and chill for several hours, turning the chops occasionally. Bring to room temperature before cooking.

Cook 2–3 minutes a side on a hot barbecue plate, anoint with more of the marinade, then finish off over the barbecue grill rack. The flames should leap and lick the chops, singeing the outside and impregnating them with smoke. Cook 2–3 minutes over the flaring grill then transfer to a serving plate. Sprinkle generously with salt then leave the chops to settle for 10 minutes before serving.

Irene's Fried Green Tomatoes

Serves 8

Remember to prepare these about 2 hours before you cook them.

8 large unripe green tomatoes
salt
½ cup flour
extra virgin olive oil

Wash and dry the tomatoes. Cut them into slices 1.5 cm thick and sprinkle on both sides with salt. Arrange them on a wire cake rack and leave to drain for 1 hour, then turn them and drain a further hour. Just prior to cooking, pat them very dry with absorbent kitchen paper. Put the flour on a plate.

Pour a 1 cm depth of oil into a large heavy-based frypan. Heat the oil over a high heat. When it is shimmering and starting to haze, quickly coat about half the tomatoes with flour then lower them into the oil. Cook until golden on both sides, then remove them with a slotted spatula, transferring them to a serving plate. Sprinkle with salt and serve hot. Continue with the rest of the tomatoes.

CANNELLINI BEAN PURÉE

SERVES 8

400 g dried cannellini beans
3 sprigs fresh sage leaves
³/₄ teaspoon salt
45 ml (3 tablespoons) olio santo (see page 114)

Put the beans in a bowl and cover generously with cold water. Leave to soak for 12 hours. Drain, rinse well then tip into a saucepan. Pour on enough cold water to cover the beans by 3 cm. Bring to a gentle boil. Boil for 5 minutes, skimming, then lower the heat, add the sage leaves, partially cover with a lid and cook gently until tender; about 1¹/₂ hours.

Drain (reserve some of the cooking liquid), discard the sage, then transfer the beans to the bowl of a food processor and process with the salt until smooth and creamy. Let the cooking liquid settle, pour off all the thin liquid and use enough of the thick liquid to turn the mixture into a fluffy purée.

The beans can be prepared ahead to this point; transfer to a bowl and cover with a piece of absorbent paper to stop the purée becoming dry on top.

Reheat the bean purée slowly in a saucepan, stirring often, then transfer it to a heated serving dish. If using the olio santo, warm it in a small frying pan and pour it over the purée. Serve immediately.

Clockwise from top right: Braised Red Onions; Marcella's Potatoes; Pork Chops with Fennel and Rosemary; Irene's Fried Green Tomatoes; Cannellini Bean Purée; Rabbit and Quail on the Barbecue

BRAISED RED ONIONS

SERVES 8

500 g red onions, peeled
50 ml extra virgin olive oil
125 ml dry white wine
1 teaspoon fennel seeds
1 teaspoon sugar
$^1/_4$ teaspoon salt
freshly ground black pepper to taste

Cut the onions in half through the root then into slices cutting through the root again. Put them in a saucepan with the oil and cook gently for 5–7 minutes, stirring occasionally, until they start to soften. Pour in the wine, add the fennel seeds, sugar, salt and pepper.

Partially cover with a lid and cook gently for 10 minutes by which time the onion should be tender and most of the liquid evaporated. Serve hot.

MARCELLA'S POTATOES

SERVES 8

$^3/_4$ teaspoon salt
freshly ground black pepper
$1^1/_2$ tablespoons dried oregano, crumbled
1.5 kg small even-sized potatoes, scrubbed
2 tablespoons extra virgin olive oil

Mix the salt, pepper and oregano on a plate.

Make deep slits in the potatoes and use a knife to spread the seasoning mixture inside the slits. Put the potatoes in a shallow-sided ovenproof dish (I use a non-stick Swiss roll tin) and drizzle with olive oil. Cook 30–40 minutes, or till tender, in an oven preheated to 200°C, shaking the pan occasionally to turn the potatoes. Serve immediately.

Zuccotto

---

60 g blanched almonds
60 g hazelnuts
175 ml coffee liqueur (or hazelnut liqueur)
150 g Savoiardi (Ladyfingers) or boudoir biscuits
350 ml cream
25 g icing sugar (depending on the sweetness of the chocolate)
1 tablespoon cocoa, sifted
90 g dark unsweetened chocolate, chopped (about $^1/_2$ cup — or use chocolate chips)
1 single round chocolate sponge, about 175 g (or extra Savoiardi biscuits)
extra coffee or hazelnut liqueur (optional)

Put the almonds in a shallow ovenproof dish and toast them in an oven preheated to 180°C for about 8 minutes, or until lightly browned. Repeat the process with the hazelnuts, cooking them about 10 minutes, or until a golden colour is visible through the burst skins. Rub vigorously in a clean cloth to remove skins. Chop the almonds and hazelnuts coarsely.

Choose a round-bottomed pudding basin with a capacity of 1.25–1.75 ml. Line the basin with plastic food wrap. Put the liqueur on a plate and dip the biscuits in the liqueur, one by one, then attach them to the inside of the bowl, sugared side outwards. Plug up any holes with small soaked pieces of biscuit. Chill.

Whip the cream until only just stiff, mix in sifted icing sugar and divide the cream in two. Mix the nuts into one bowl of cream, and the cocoa and chocolate into the other. Chill the chocolate cream. Spread the nut cream evenly round the sides over the biscuits, taking care not to dislodge any. Leave a cavity in the centre for the second mixture. Chill.

Spoon the chocolate cream into the centre. Put the round of sponge on top (splash with a little extra liqueur if liked) and push down lightly. Alternatively, arrange Savoiardi biscuits on top. Cover with plastic wrap and refrigerate overnight.

When ready to serve, invert carefully onto a plate. If the plastic wrap is still attached, peel it off. Dust the top with icing sugar. Alternatively cut out strips of paper and decorate the top with alternate stripes of sifted cocoa and icing sugar.

LA PRIMAVERA

After several months with Remo, I went over to London to do a cookery course at the Cordon Bleu Cookery School. It was a good test for us both. We were distraught at being apart, it was wretched, and once school finished I returned to Genova to live with him. He proposed on bended knees. What was a girl to do? The word 'yes' was out of my mouth before I knew it. We planned to stay in Genova that year then go to New Zealand for Christmas. But things didn't quite work out that way.

Around September the tide started turning. It would be spring in New Zealand — a good time to return. For the first time Remo expressed doubts about coming to New Zealand. I panicked. I hadn't been home for nearly three years. I missed my mum. I was going. Although there were many things I loved about Italy, I knew I couldn't marry, have children and make my life there. I was my own person. I didn't want to lose my identity, be driven around by men, have decisions made for me by men and spend half my day cooking and cleaning for men.

It's a terrible tale to tell but in Remo's family, which is not at all out of the ordinary, the women shopped for and cooked the food. They set the table for meals, then cleared the table after meals and did the dishes. Not a look-in from the men. The worst bit was sweeping the floor. The men would remain at the table while the cleaning was done, sipping on coffee and digestives and smoking, and they would help the women by raising their feet when the broom came their way. How bloody helpful, I always thought. (This was 20 years ago — things have changed dramatically with the younger generation.)

I knew I would explode at such unfairness and our relationship wouldn't stand a chance. I didn't know what the future would hold for us in New Zealand, but I was sure it would be better than in Italy. These were tough times: Remo wasn't coming; I wasn't staying. I booked my ticket home, knowing once I had done that I wouldn't back down.

My last week in Genova in December 1977 was a sad one. Remo moved away. He just couldn't cope with my imminent departure. His family was fantastic and helped me pack and organise, all the things Remo would have helped with but couldn't because of his personal pain. Mysteriously, our cat Humphrey went missing that week too and never returned home.

I was to travel by train to London. I went to the Biuso family home for a goodbye meal which we consumed around the long table, the dining table which had been so central to my life with Remo. Everyone was in low spirits.

Roasted Potatoes with Sea
Salt; Zucchini Trifolati; Lamb
Cutlets with Sweet
Capsicums; La Frittedda

Unexpectedly Remo turned up. We took one look at each other and burst into tears. It was dreadful, truly dreadful. I said tearful goodbyes to his family, not knowing whether I would see them again, then Remo accompanied me to the train station.

It was one of the most difficult times of my life. A time of utmost confusion. I knew I had to go, for my sake, for our sakes if there was to be a future, but it didn't make it any easier. A sad parting at a railway station is wrenching. We were so hopelessly in love.

My last glimpse as the train pulled out of Genova was of Remo, his sister Marcella and husband Alberto hugging each other. I took a couple of sniffs of Mamma Rosa's picnic pack of potato frittata for comfort and a slug from Papà Michele's carafe to steel my nerves. Oh God, I thought, why am I leaving?

It took Remo six weeks to make up his mind and nearly six months to settle his affairs and move to New Zealand. He gave up his job, his apartment and his friends to make a new life with me on the other side of the world. He was a brave man. At least I knew where I was going and where I didn't want to be. Going to New Zealand, he later told me, was like going to the moon. We had to agree to marry, of course: that was a little technicality the government imposed upon us in order for him to get his visa. This we did in February 1979 — just as the first signs of spring were showing in Italy.

SHAKING OFF THE WINTER BLUES

Italians are seriously keen on spring. After they've huddled inside out of the cold for months, the warmer weather brings them forth in a flurry of activity. It's time to shake off the winter blues and to celebrate new life.

Easter is a reason to be joyous, and a time for the family to rekindle bonds around the feast table. The marketplace is once again a good place to be. Shoppers dawdle happily among the stalls gossiping with their favoured stallholders and basking in the warmer air.

Baby peas and broad beans make a fleeting appearance and are snapped up by home cooks, mostly women, keen to capture the sweet peas or milky beans in their favourite handed-down family recipes. Mounds of tightly budded small artichokes with their spiky tips tinged with purple hues lie waiting for stallholders to execute their measured 'chop and trim' technique as they prepare them to order.

Asparagus, fat-tipped, green, mauve-tinged and white; unblemished crisp white and green striped bulbs of fennel with feathery manes waving in the breeze; baby herbs bundled up in soggy wrappings of recycled brown paper or newspaper, bound with rubber bands, fill the market with nose-turning aromas. Pale, rosy baby lamb, with the tenderest meat, is a paschal treat not to be missed. Citrus fruits mingle on stalls with red, black and blueberries, glossy cherries and blushing apricots the first of the stone fruits.

Ah, the market in spring is a stimulating place for the cook.

The stallholders expect to sell you something. They're cheekier than usual. They know that spring makes even the poor forgo their frugality, and the rich their parsimonious ways. They flirt with the frugal, teasing them with tempting produce till they weaken and buy; and they pinch from the rich, inflating prices under their very noses. It's all irresistible to watch, to be part of.

The one o'clock dinner gong comes too soon, and urgent last-minute purchases are pushed through at double or half the price, depending on the skill of the haggler. Then that's business over for another day. Shutters are pulled down on shop fronts, tarpaulins slung over wooden stalls. Within ten minutes of closing, the market is like a ghost town and remains so until the dawn of a new day brings it to life again.

Vegetables and fruit in Italy still clearly reflect the seasonal cycles, but these days you will find imported vegetables and fruits in the marketplace. While there are many culinary changes taking place in Italy, one aspect I hope will never change is the affinity the Italians have with the seasons.

Some Notes on Vegetables

Vegetables are probably the most misunderstood part of the Italian menu.

In the western world, no sooner had we shrugged off boiled-to-death cabbage and soggy carrots, and embraced crunchy vegetables, than the rage for Italian food, with, you guessed it, soggy vegetables, came along.

Before Italian food was fashionable, the two most common complaints about it were that it was too oily and that the vegetables were overcooked. We've now come to appreciate that the oil slick on the food is deliberate, and is there, not because Italians like their food oily, but because it adds flavour and enriches dishes with nutrients and makes them palatable.

There's a good case to make for Italian vegetables too. The usual western way is to boil vegetables in water, drain them and serve them. The Italians have another agenda; nothing is thrown away, particularly vegetable water, which contains flavour and nutrients.

Instead of drowning vegetables in a big pot of water, they put them in a pot with just enough water to barely cover them, or enough to bubble away and create steam. Olive oil and garlic might be added to the vegetables, along with herbs and seasonings. As the water evaporates, a little more is added; the vegetables are never flooded with it. The last of the water is allowed to bubble away and amalgamate with the oil forming a light sheen or dressing on the vegetables. They emerge bursting with flavour — all their flavour, as none is poured down the sink. The vegetables are tender and digestible and full of nutrients.

Consider broccoli. The Italians steam or cook it till it is very tender. It is then mashed to a lumpy pale green purée in a large frypan with loads of extra virgin olive oil and lashings of crushed garlic. It tastes superb — nutty and creamy.

Quickly blanched, crunchy asparagus is delicious with melted butter or a vinaigrette — but hopeless in a frittata or risotto. Crunchy asparagus will split a frittata and is at odds with its tender texture. In a risotto you want the asparagus to nestle into the rice grains, for the whole dish to be meltingly creamy; if it was crunchy, the asparagus would separate from the mass of rice grains and you'd still be masticating the fibres long after the creamy rice had slid down your throat.

There's nothing wrong with crunchy broccoli or asparagus — they just don't belong in or with Italian dishes.

Some Tips and Information

Artichokes

Always use a stainless steel knife (not a carbon one) to cut artichokes; carbon taints them, causing blackening to the artichoke and the knife (if you accidentally use a carbon steel knife, clean it after with half a lemon; it will remove the black and the nasty metallic smell).

Preparing artichokes

There are several ways to prepare an artichoke. First, fill a bowl with water and squeeze the juice of a lemon into it. As the artichokes are prepared, put them in the water; the lemon will help prevent them discolouring. It's a good idea to wear thin food preparation gloves when preparing artichokes to prevent them staining the hands.

Cut off the top third of the artichoke and discard (the tips of the leaves). Trim the stalk; if it is very fibrous, peel the outside of it. The artichoke can be boiled as it is, and the choke removed after cooking; this is suitable when artichokes are to be served cold, but does not apply to any recipes in this book. If you want to cook the artichoke with seasoning or stuffing, spread the leaves apart, opening and loosening the trimmed artichoke. Remove the mauve-coloured leaves in the centre, then press the soft, yellowish leaves away from the centre until a cavity is formed and the choke is revealed. The choke is a collection of fibrous hairs, which should be totally scraped out as it is inedible, even after cooking. Use a pointed teaspoon to remove it, but take care to remove only the hairy fibre, because directly below this is the meaty base of the artichoke (referred to as the fond or heart). The artichoke is then ready for seasoning or stuffing.

A delicious Roman treatment is to rub them with an oily dressing of chopped garlic, olive oil, salt, pepper and mint and steam them in a little water and some more of the dressing till tender. When they are ready, transfer them to a plate, stems up, and reduce the juices until an emulsion forms. Pour this over the artichokes and serve them at room temperature.

When the artichokes are to be sliced, as they are in the recipes for Artichoke Frittata (page 96) and La Frittedda (page 64), it is easier to cut off the tips, slice the artichoke in half and extract the half-choke, then slice thinly.

Jerusalem artichokes

The Jerusalem artichoke, a native to North America, looks like a gnarled piece of fresh ginger and has an interesting, nutty-earthy flavour. They are not related to globe artichokes although some say there is a similarity of taste. They tend to darken once peeled or cut, but putting them into lightly acidulated water (water to which lemon juice or vinegar has been added) during preparation, or cooking them in either acidulated water or milk, lessens the discolouration. They make a delicious soup, a good purée, can be boiled and dressed with olive oil and served as a salad, or made into chips (page 153).

Roasting capsicums

Roasting capsicums over a gas flame, a hot barbecue or in the oven causes the skin to char and blister, making it easy to remove. The charring brings out a nutty, sweet, slightly smoky flavour.

They can be used immediately, or kept for several days, covered and refrigerated. They are delicious drizzled with extra virgin olive oil, on their own or flecked with herbs, or dotted with capers, olives, anchovy pieces etc. Serve as a nibble or atop pizzas or crostini.

Skinning tomatoes

When tomatoes are eaten fresh, as in a salad, there is usually no need to remove the skins (unless they are tough) but if the tomatoes are to be used in soups, sauces or vegetable stews it is advisable to do so. The skin tends to separate from the flesh during cooking and float to the surface, looking unappetising and tasting tough. Also, cooked tomato skins are not easily digested.

The idea is to immerse the tomato in hot water so it swells. This makes the skin taut and causes it to burst. Drop the tomatoes into a saucepan of boiling water and leave for 12–20 seconds, depending on how ripe they are. Lift out the tomatoes with a slotted spoon and transfer to a bowl of cold water. If the tomato is difficult to peel, repeat the process. If the tomato looks fluffy of furry, it was in the water too long and has started to cook; cut the seconds down for any further tomatoes.

Never remove the skins from tomatoes which are to be baked in the oven; it holds them together and they will collapse without it.

Tomato sauce

When tomatoes are processed, the seeds, which are bitter, are also broken down. This can make the sauce taste bitter. A mouli-légumes extracts the maximum pulp from the tomato fibre and seeds, but traps the seeds. It produces a sauce with texture and good taste.

Tomatoes — fresh versus tinned

There is no point in making a tomato sauce with hot-house or unripe tomatoes because it will be a let-down — either pale and watery, or insipid, or acid, or all of these. Use tomatoes ripened on the vine, which have a fresh fruit flavour, and choose a fleshier type: what you need for a good sauce is pulp, not water.

If vine-ripened tomatoes are not available (and they are seasonal), use Italian canned tomatoes, preferably the San Marzanno variety. These tomatoes, packed in their own juice, not brine, capture something of the wonderful summer flavour of fresh outdoor tomatoes, and will make a sauce of good colour, aroma, consistency and taste.

Storing mushrooms

If given the option of buying mushrooms in a plastic bag or in a brown paper bag, always choose the latter. Mushrooms stored in plastic (at room temperature or in the fridge) quickly sweat or become moist, then turn soggy and rot.

Store them either in an unsealed brown paper bag or unsealed in a large plastic bag or container lined with absorbent kitchen paper.

To chop or crush garlic

Garlic is traditionally chopped, not crushed. If you're curious about this, just remember that Italians were cooking with garlic long before garlic crushers were invented. In most recipes the difference is hard to detect, but when it is, as in Isanna's Eggs page 91, where the pungent zing of chopped raw garlic is an integral part of the dish and the element which stops the egg yolks and oil becoming too rich, I suggest you prepare it this way. Chopped garlic is stronger probably because you use more of it and the pieces are bigger when they hit your palate. If you want a milder taste, use crushed garlic and less of it.

Under no circumstances should you use the last of the season's garlic raw in a dish — if the garlic has started to sprout (small pale green sprout in the centre of the clove) it will repeat on you after eating it. Garlic crushers usually catch the sprout but if you want to remove it by hand, cut the clove in half and pick it out.

Steaming vegetables

Less nutrients are lost when vegetables are cooked above, rather than in, boiling water. Steaming also preserves more of the flavour and structure of the vegetables. This is particularly noticeable with new potatoes. However, green vegetables, such as beans and broccoli, lose their bright green appealing colour when steamed.

Dried herbs

Fresh herbs are bulkier than dried and dried herbs are more concentrated than fresh. My advice when using dried herbs is to use half or slightly less than half the fresh quantity (eg 1 tablespoon chopped marjoram = $^1/_2$ tablespoon dried marjoram, crumbled).

Rubbing dried herbs in the palms of the hands not only breaks the herbs into smallish, manageable bits, but the warmth of the palms seems to draw out the oils, or remaining aromas of the herbs. Highly recommended for the sniff value if nothing else!

Light feathery herbs, such as fennel, do not dry well; nor does basil.

Porcini (cèpe)

Porcini or *cèpe* (*Boletus edulis*) is an edible fungus, available fresh in Europe during the autumn months, or dried at other times of the year. Usually only dried *Boletus* are exported. Dried, they possess a woodsy aroma with a savoury concentrated flavour. They give a full mushroom flavour to everything they are cooked with.

Reconstitute them by soaking for 30 minutes in water. Put the porcini in a sieve and rinse under running water. Tip them into a bowl and pour on the specified amount of hot water. Leave to soak for 30 minutes, then lift them out of the liquid using a slotted spoon and transfer to a sieve (reserve the soaking liquid). Rinse well under running water then chop finely, discarding any woody bits. Strain the soaking liquid into a bowl through a sieve lined with a piece of absorbent paper. Strain again and use as required.

SALADS

Preparing salad greens

If you enjoy salads, get yourself a salad spinner. These usually work on a centrifugal system; a salad basket is spun around a bowl by a pull-handle and any water on the greens placed in the basket is spun out. It's an excellent method for drying washed salad greens and herbs, causing little damage.

The old Italian trick of bundling the salad items in a clean cloth and shaking it vigorously out the window is 'kinda quaint' but bruises the leaves beyond repair.

Once the leaves are dried they can be kept crisp by transferring them to a plastic bag and chilling them in the fridge for an hour, or several hours, but it is best not to tear the leaves into bite-size pieces until assembling the salad.

Salad dressings

The amount of salt required in an oil-based dressing is often not stated. The recipe will probably read 'salt to taste' and that's because it depends on the type and quality of oil used, and to a lesser degree, on the type of salt. The heavier oils, like olive oil and peanut oil, require more salt than light oils such as safflower oil. Oils also differ from brand to brand.

Although an oil-based dressing may 'taste' of the oil used (for example, olivey or fruity if made from olive oil, or nutty if made from a nut oil) it should never actually be oily or greasy.

Salt, with its slight abrasiveness, has the effect of cutting through the oil texture in a dressing (as well as flavouring the food). To illustrate this, smear a little oil on your palms, then rub them together. They will feel smooth and slippery. Now sprinkle on a little salt and rub them together again. You'll notice the salt's abrasiveness and how it gets rid of the slippery feeling. Imagine this on your palate.

Add salt to dressings by degrees, say 2–3 pinches. Whisk it in, let it settle a few minutes, then whisk again. It should be smooth, but it shouldn't leave your mouth coated in oil. If you over-salt the dressing, dilute it with more oil and readjust the acid content.

Pesto Secret

If you have ever eaten a bowl of pasta dressed with an oil-based sauce such as pesto, which starts out tasting delicious, but half-way through it goes sort of heavy and oily, and the more cheese you put on, the tackier and less appetising it becomes, read on.

• First, don't over-drain the pasta; leave a fair amount of moisture clinging to it (I'm talking noodles here). If you over-drain it, the heat dries the surface of the pasta and the sauce sinks in instead of sliding over and coating the pasta — basil pesto actually stains the pasta.
• Toss the drained pasta with a little butter to flavour it and to help the sauce flow over.
• Dilute the pesto, not with more oil, which would throw out the balance of flavours and make the pesto too oily on the palate, but with a little of the hot pasta water (it brings up the colour too). Toss pesto and pasta and add enough hot pasta water (1–3 tablespoons) to enable the pesto to flow easily over the pasta. You may shake your head in disbelief at the idea of adding hot pasta water, but the result is delicious beyond description.
• If you're cooking tubular shapes, which can trap a lot of water inside them, give the colander a quick jerk which shoots this water out, but make the overall draining operation as brief as for noodles, so the outside surface of the pasta doesn't dry completely.

LA PRIMAVERA

SERVES 6

Francesco's Artichoke and Orange Salad

Genovese Spring Pasta
or
Risotto with Asparagus as made in Reggio Emilia

Lamb Cutlets with Sweet Capsicums
Roasted Potatoes with Sea Salt
Zucchini Trifolati
La Frittedda

Tiziana's Lemon and Almond Cake

This menu makes the most of spring vegetables, citrus fruit and young lamb. The starter, ARTICHOKE AND ORANGE SALAD, is the creation of a Florentine chef, Francesco Visani, whom I met in New Zealand when he was doing a chef stint in Auckland. Fresh artichokes are lovely treated this way but any good quality artichokes preserved in oil can be used (the preserving brine used in most canned artichokes is too strong and makes them unsuitable). I like the contrast of fresh sweet oranges and the earthy taste of the artichokes lifted with a fruity olive oil and the welcome salty bite of prosciutto. Quite clever really. Colonna mandarin-infused extra virgin olive oil, or the regular Colonna extra virgin olive oil, are my preference for this dish.

Most fans of Italian food will have eaten pesto and pasta in various shapes and forms, but this exquisite SPRING PASTA dish, a specialty of Genova, takes the process a step further. When it is properly executed, it is stunning. You need to have all the elements right.

First, choose waxy new potatoes and cook them in their skins. Use fresh snappy beans, the thinnest you can find, and cook them until tender; crisp, crunchy beans will be at odds with the texture of the pasta. Make your own pesto — it takes all of five minutes in a machine (if you have the time, crush the basil in a mortar and pestle because it extracts more flavour from the basil — a processor merely chops it — and produces a superior sauce.) Use quality Italian pasta, parmigiano reggiano, and romano cheese, if available. With excellent ingredients, it's an easy enough dish to put together.

If you're serving the artichoke starter, bring the potatoes to the boil just before serving it. They can then be left to cook gently while you're eating it and will be ready for you to carry on with the recipe once you've finished it. That's if you have opted for the pasta.

RISOTTO with the first of the season's asparagus is something the Italians look forward to with joy. The beauty of the dish is its melting creaminess offset against the chew of the rice, the delicacy of young asparagus, cooked until it softens and nestles into the rice grains, teased by piquant notes of parmesan cheese here and there and the glorious richness fresh butter brings to the dish when whipped in at the end. A real joy to create and eat.

Don't make it a home for crunchy asparagus, or improperly cooked rice, or for any other rice than Italian risotto rice (*arborio, carnaroli, vialone nano*). I sometimes wish that all those people who create such abominations in the name of classic dishes and cooking methods could try things properly done just once in their lives; it would revolutionise their approach to cooking.

If you choose the risotto, you can partly prepare it ahead — up to the point where the wine is added — which will make finishing it off a little quicker.

The LAMB course is a stand-alone meal should you not want any preceding courses, or, alternatively, precede it with the artichoke salad only. (Both the pasta and risotto dishes are substantial enough to serve as main courses some other time if you wish, perhaps followed by salad, cheese and fruit: the risotto will serve 4, the pasta 4–6.)

The POTATOES which accompany the lamb are a Biuso favourite. What easier way is there to produce crisp, crunchy potatoes than cubing them, putting them in a roasting dish with oil and butter and cooking them for 45 minutes; no soggy potatoes, no spitting fat, just crisp crunch. Yum!

The ZUCCHINI recipe is something to treasure. Vegetables cooked by this method, known as *trifolati*, are usually quickly fried in olive oil with garlic and finished with plenty of chopped parsley — but there are variations, such as this zucchini dish which is cooked in butter. The onion becomes golden and sweet in the butter and the sweetness permeates the zucchini. The trick is to have the heat high to drive off most of the moisture but not all of it, so the zucchini can continue to brown but because the pan isn't totally dry, the onion and garlic won't burn.

It's such a simple and delicious way of cooking zucchini that it's often hard to consider any other treatment for this vegetable. If you can master this recipe you can make a meal of it with crunchy bread, a decent salad and a jug of wine at some time when you want a casual tasty repast. You are aiming for totally tender discs of zucchini — keep crunchy vegetables for another night! If you want to serve the zucchini at room temperature, it's better to cook them in olive oil.

LA FRITTEDDA is a glorious tangle of spring vegetables. Originating in Sicily, La Frittedda may be presented as a mash of spring vegetables. I prefer the vegetables to retain their identity. It's gorgeous with the lamb. If you've chosen Francesco's artichoke recipe, I would substitute a salad for La Frittedda, as a double-up of artichokes is a bit excessive. Flicking the outer skins off the broad beans is tedious, but well worth it.

The LEMON CAKE would keep you full in the trenches, or at times when you need to rely on your reserves; that is, until the lemon syrup is poured over it. Boy, does that change it. It retains the almond crunch, and some almond flavour, but it becomes much lighter to eat, much fresher of course, and much more interesting. Although it should feed many more than six people, sometimes, if you haven't had a huge meal in front of it, six greedy people can gobble it up at an incredible rate, with glazed strawberries too. And who is Tiziana? My sister-in-law Isanna's nextdoor neighbour, who makes excellent cakes.

So, you've been warned in detail about this menu. The artichoke and orange dish could be a light starter to many a different meal. The Ligurian pasta and Emilian risotto can be exquisite, but if you are in the mood for shortcuts, look elsewhere. The lamb can be cooked inside or outdoors, the potatoes are a doddle and the zucchini have to be tried to be believed. I leave the SALAD up to you (if you are buying ready-picked and washed salad leaves, go organic and buy leaves which have not been washed in chlorine — oh, you didn't know that that is what stops the cut ends from going brown?). As far as the cake is concerned, just remember you need seven lemons.

FRANCESCO'S ARTICHOKE AND ORANGE SALAD

SERVES 6

6 whole preserved artichokes, or 6 fresh artichokes, or 2 cups canned or
bottled artichokes in olive oil (do not use artichokes in brine)
45 ml (3 tablespoons) extra virgin olive oil, or
Colonna mandarin-infused extra virgin olive oil
¼ teaspoon salt
15 ml (1 tablespoon) white wine vinegar — tarragon-flavoured is good
freshly ground black pepper to taste
3–4 juicy oranges, peeled and segmented
1 tablespoon coarsely chopped Italian parsley
100 g air-dried or cured meat such as bresaola, capocollo, prosciutto

If using preserved artichokes, drain them and slice thinly. If using fresh artichokes, prepare them and steam till tender (see page 50). If using canned or bottled artichoke hearts, drain and slice thinly (these are not as attractive to look at as the other two options, but do the trick tastewise).

Mix the olive oil, salt, vinegar and black pepper together in a large bowl. Add the artichokes and oranges and toss gently. Leave to marinate for 30 minutes.

Before serving, add the parsley, toss and arrange on plates. Garnish with the meat and serve with crusty bread.

Francesco's Artichoke and Orange Salad

GENOVESE SPRING PASTA

SERVES 6–8

2 cups fresh basil leaves, tightly packed
salt
2 cloves garlic, chopped
3 tablespoons pinenuts
45 ml (3 tablespoons) extra virgin olive oil
4 tablespoons freshly grated parmesan cheese
2 tablespoons freshly grated romano cheese (if not available,
use 6 tablespoons of parmesan cheese)
150 g (about 3) small new potatoes (choose a waxy or salad variety)
200 g young, slim green beans, topped and tailed, and halved if long
600 g spaghettini (or use trenette, spaghetti or linguine)
50 g butter

PESTO

Make the pesto in a food processor: put the basil leaves, a pinch of salt, garlic, pinenuts and oil in the processor bowl fitted with the steel chopping blade and process the mixture till blended. Transfer to a bowl then mix in the cheeses by hand. Cover the surface with plastic wrap and set aside until required.

Scrub the potatoes, put in a saucepan with cold, salted water and bring to the boil. Lower the heat and cook gently until just tender. Drain, and when cool enough to handle, peel and slice thinly.

Once the potatoes are nearly done, put the pasta water on to boil. Cook the beans by plunging them into a pan of boiling, salted water and cooking gently until just tender. Drain, rinse and set aside.

Cook the spaghettini in plenty of boiling, well-salted water until al dente. Drain briefly, reserving a cup of the pasta cooking water, then tip the pasta into a heated serving bowl and quickly toss through the butter. Add 2 tablespoons of the reserved pasta water to the pesto, then toss it through the pasta, adding about ¼ cup more of the pasta water, to give the sauce a light consistency. Add the beans and potatoes, toss briefly, then serve immediately.

Serves 6

450 g new season's asparagus
salt
approximately 1500 ml stock (include some asparagus cooking water)
45 ml (3 tablespoons) olive oil
75 g fresh unsalted butter
half a small onion, finely chopped
1 large clove garlic, crushed
400 g Italian risotto rice (arborio, carnaroli, vialone nano)
125 ml (¹/₂ cup) dry white wine
freshly ground black pepper to taste
50 g (¹/₂ cup) freshly grated parmesan cheese, plus extra for serving

Trim the asparagus and wash it well. Plunge it into a saucepan of salted boiling water and cook for 7 minutes. Drain, reserving some of the cooking water, and refresh it with cold water. Leave to drain, then chop it into short lengths.

Bring the stock to a slow, steady simmer (include some of the reserved cooking water), then lower the heat so that it stops simmering but stays very hot (if it boils, it will evaporate).

Choose a cast-iron casserole or heavy-based saucepan with a 3-litre capacity. Set it over a moderate heat, pour in the oil and add half the butter, then add the onion and garlic. Sauté until a pale golden colour, then add the asparagus. Cook 1–2 minutes, stirring well.

Tip in the rice and stir thoroughly. Add the white wine, cook for 3–4 minutes, then start adding the stock (2 ladlefuls to begin with). Stir gently but continuously until the stock has nearly evaporated. Continue cooking in this way for 10–12 minutes, adding stock as required and stirring continuously to stop the rice sticking.

The rice is ready when the grains are al dente — still firm and only just cooked through, but no longer chalky inside (this is a moot point — some of my Italian family like the rice quite undercooked). It will take around 20 minutes to cook. Season with ¹/₂ teaspoon of salt and plenty of black pepper, then whip in the rest of the butter and the parmesan cheese. Cover with a lid and leave to infuse for 2 minutes. Serve immediately in hot bowls, accompanied by extra parmesan cheese.

Lamb Cutlets with Sweet Capsicums

Serves 6

3 red capsicums
extra virgin olive oil
1 teaspoon red wine vinegar
salt
freshly ground black pepper to taste
18–24 small lamb cutlets, well trimmed (these should be rosy in colour,
taken from racks of young lamb and thinly cut, with all fat trimmed)
60 ml (4 tablespoons) olive oil
2 large anchovy fillets
1 large clove garlic, finely chopped
1 tiny dried bird's-eye chilli, crushed
2 tablespoons finely chopped Italian parsley
1 teaspoon finely chopped marjoram

Prepare the capsicums as described on page 50. When cool, peel off the skin and remove the cores and seeds. Cut the capsicums into large chunks and place in a shallow ovenproof serving dish. Pour on any juices and sprinkle with 1 teaspoon extra virgin olive oil and the vinegar, a sprinkling of salt and some black pepper.

Cook the cutlets in batches. Heat half the olive oil in a large heavy-based frypan and fry half the cutlets briskly on both sides till brown (cook a few minutes each side; the cutlets should be pink and juicy inside). Transfer the cutlets to a plate and sprinkle each with salt. Repeat the procedure with the rest of the cutlets. Allow the frying pan to cool briefly, then pour off most of the oil, leaving any sediment. Splash in 4 tablespoons of water then add the anchovy fillets, 1 tablespoon extra virgin olive oil, the garlic, chilli, parsley and marjoram. Simmer very gently, mashing the anchovy fillets into the sauce. Transfer the capsicums to a heated serving dish and arrange the cutlets on top, spoon over the juices from the frypan and serve immediately.

If frying the cutlets inside sounds hellish to you, then cook them outside on a barbecue (or get someone else to cook them) and make the sauce separately. Prepare the cutlets, put them in a dish and pour over ¼ cup olive oil (the extra oil is necessary or the cutlets may burn and be dry to eat) and grind on some black pepper. Cook for a few minutes each side on a hot (preheated) barbecue plate or grill rack; they should be nice and pink inside. Transfer them to a plate and sprinkle with salt; drain briefly before serving. Transfer the capsicums to a heated plate and arrange the cutlets on top.

Have ready the anchovies mashed to a paste in a small frypan with the oil, garlic and chilli; this can be prepared an hour or so in advance. When the cutlets are nearly done, gently heat the anchovy mixture — don't let it fry or the anchovies will go into premature rigor mortis. Add four tablespoons of the reserved pepper juices and the parsley and pour over the cutlets and capsicums.

Roasted Potatoes with Sea Salt

Serves 6

1500 g roasting potatoes, peeled and cubed
50 ml olive oil
³/₄ teaspoon sea salt flakes
50 g butter
2 large cloves garlic, finely chopped

Put the potato cubes in a large shallow oven dish. Pour on the olive oil, sprinkle on the salt and dot with butter. Roast about 45 minutes in an oven preheated to 200°C, turning often; the potatoes will probably stick a bit to the dish, but this doesn't matter as the stuck bits will loosen at the end of cooking and become very crisp.

When the potatoes are golden (this may take longer than 45 minutes), sprinkle over the chopped garlic. Stir the garlic through and return the potatoes to the oven for about 7 minutes more, or until the garlic is lightly browned (do not overcook or the garlic will darken and taste bitter). Serve immediately with all the scrapings.

Lamb Cutlets with Sweet Capsicums, Zucchini Trifolati,
La Frittedda and Roasted Potatoes with Sea Salt

Zucchini Trifolati

Serves 4–6

700 g slim zucchini, finely sliced
50 g butter
1 large onion, finely chopped
1 large clove garlic, finely chopped
$^1/_4$ teaspoon salt and freshly ground black pepper to taste

Wash the zucchini, pat dry then trim and slice very thinly. Melt the butter in a large heavy-based frypan over medium heat and add the onion. Cook gently until the onion just starts to turn golden, then increase the heat to medium-high and add the zucchini. Stir well to coat with the buttery onion, add the garlic then cook until the zucchini discs are very tender and lightly golden; the onion should be a rich golden colour. If the mixture starts to burn, lower the heat. Stir through the salt and pepper and transfer to a serving dish. Serve hottish.

La Frittedda

Serves 8

1 kg fresh broad beans or 500 g frozen broad beans
salt
2 fennel bulbs, with feathery tops attached
1 kg fresh peas in their pods or 300 g frozen baby peas
200 g asparagus
75 ml (5 tablespoons) extra virgin olive oil
1 large red onion, very finely sliced
freshly ground black pepper to taste
2 young artichokes, prepared and cooked as in the recipe for artichoke frittata (page 96),
or 300 g jar artichoke pieces in olive oil (buy an imported Italian brand)

Pod the broad beans. If using frozen broad beans, tip them into a saucepan of boiling salted water. Cover with a lid, quickly bring to the boil, then drain and refresh with plenty of cold water. When cool enough to touch, flick off the outer skins and discard.

Trim the fennel, setting aside the feathery tops. Cut the fennel bulbs into quarters, wash, shake dry and slice finely, discarding the cores. Chop the feathery tops. Pod the peas. If using frozen peas, put them in a large colander and rinse with hot water until the ice crystals disappear. Wash and trim the asparagus, and cut on the diagonal into three pieces.

Put the oil and onion in a large heavy-based frypan over a low heat. Cook very gently until the onion has softened; it should smell sweet and look translucent. If using fresh broad beans and peas, add them now. Add 3 tablespoons of water and cook gently, covered with a lid, for 10 minutes. Add the asparagus pieces, stir well then cover with a lid and cook gently for 5 minutes. Tip in the fennel, cook another 5 minutes, covered, then add

$^1/_2$ teaspoon salt, pepper and the artichokes. If using frozen beans or peas, add them now.

Cook uncovered 5–10 minutes more, or till the vegetables are done to your liking. Sprinkle over half a cup of the chopped feathery fennel leaves, stir in, then transfer to a serving bowl. Serve hot.

A few pea pods added to the mix will give the vegetables a lovely sweet flavour.

TIZIANA'S LEMON AND ALMOND CAKE

$^1/_2$ cup milk
1 tablespoon dried yeast
3 eggs, at room temperature
200 g castor sugar
125 ml ($^1/_2$ cup) light oil
100 g unblanched almonds, finely chopped
grated rind of 1 lemon
300 g flour
pinch of salt
icing sugar

SYRUP
8 tablespoons castor sugar
juice of 6 lemons, strained

Heat the milk in a small saucepan (or in the microwave) until just warm to the little finger. Sprinkle over the yeast and set aside while preparing the other ingredients; stir occasionally. Break the eggs into the bowl of a mixer or food processor. Beat with the whisk until liquefied, then, with the machine running, pour in the castor sugar slowly. Continue beating until the mixture leaves a thick trail off the up-held beaters (the 'ribbon'); this may take 5 minutes or more.

Stir the yeast until it is dissolved, then pour into the whisked eggs, along with the oil. Add the almonds and lemon rind and mix everything together with a large spoon.

Sift one third of the flour over the surface and fold in with a large spoon, then mix in the the rest of the flour, with a pinch of salt, in two batches.

Pour into a buttered non-stick cake tin, 23 cm in diameter. Cook 30–40 minutes in an oven preheated to 180°C, until golden in colour and pulling away from the sides of the tin and springy on top. Cool the cake in the tin for 10 minutes, then loosen it from around the sides with a thin knife and invert it onto a cooling rack.

When the cake is cold, transfer it to a serving plate.

Mix the lemon juice and sugar together in a small bowl and stir until dissolved. Poke lots of small holes on the top of the cake with a skewer and carefully pour over about a third of the lemon syrup. Let the cake absorb the syrup for about half an hour then pour over another third of the syrup and let it rest another 30 minutes before pouring over the final portion of syrup. Just before serving, sprinkle the surface of the cake with icing sugar.

THE RICHES OF EMILIA-ROMAGNA

THE LOLLI FAMILY

You can call it luck if you like, I married into an Italian family with fingers in the best Italian culinary pies: Ligurian; Venetian; Tuscan; Sicilian and Emilian. I'm probably most passionate about Sicilian food, but the food from Emilia-Romagna comes a close second. My sister-in-law Isanna and her mother Gemma are responsible for my immersion into the Emilian cuisine. They are both superb cooks and many of the recipes in this book have come hot off their kitchen stoves.

When it comes to food, nothing is too much trouble. Pasta is whipped up before my eyes; rabbits are killed, hung and on the table with bread-dunking sauces within forty-eight hours of the merest hint of desiring such a dish; wild mushrooms are procured in the dawn hours by Aleardo, Isanna's father. If you even look hungry, Gemma or Isanna sling on their aprons and attach themselves to the stove and kitchen bench until they have produced some little morsel, smelling so tempting that it's impossible to resist. And resisting is silly. This food is so good, I make a beeline for their homes whenever I am in Italy.

The long lunches and celebratory meals I have enjoyed around the Lolli table (yup, that's Isanna's maiden name) could fill a book. Gastronomic blow-outs. Orgiastic feasts. Wolfish repasts. Downright gluttony. I've experienced them all in Reggio Emilia, a town in the Emilia-Romagna region, where Isanna and her family live.

A FAMILY CHRISTENING

Italians are true lovers of life. They sing, they dance and they feast, celebrating the harvest, births, marriages and saints' days. Having snatched Remo from the bosom of his *famiglia* to drag him 12,000 miles to 'the end of the earth', I felt the least I could do to appease my in-laws was to agree to have our children christened in Italy.

When our first child Luca was about ten months old we decided it was time to bring him to Italy so the family could meet him. He was christened during the summer of his first year, a wonderful day spent celebrating and feasting in the open air around a long table at the home of Isanna's parents, Gemma and Aleardo, in rural Reggio Emilia. A second child meant an obligatory return pilgrimage to Italy, which we did when Ilaria was two, but our daughter's launch into *la famiglia Italiana* was different from Luca's.

It was autumn and the fresh nip in the air made the roaring log fire in the huge family

Pumpkin Tortelli with
Chilli Sage Butter

room at Gemma and Aleardo's farmhouse much more inviting than the breezy courtyard. Warming, nourishing food was in order for the christening feast. Planning had gone on for more than a week. The spacious three-storeyed house had been spring-cleaned top to bottom; the all-important visit (and donation) had been made to the priest; a small fortune had been spent by everyone on clothes, shoes, hats, bags and hairdos and, most importantly, the menu had been decided.

When Gemma offered to make the Emilia-Romagna specialty *cappelletti in brodo* (stuffed pasta in broth), a dish reserved for celebratory meals, I was ecstatic, knowing the amount of work involved in making cappelletti for 40. A friend of Aleardo suggested one of his hand-raised pigs for a spit-roast, and along with a bounty of fresh vegetables and herbs from Aleardo's prolific vegetable garden, we had the basis for our menu.

Several days before the event, the men went out to select the pig for slaughtering and to choose the huge hunk of *parmigiano reggiano* which would be served in a large piece for everyone to nibble when the fancy took them, and which would be used in practically every dish on the menu. Aleardo has a fair amount of clout in these matters. He used to provide a local *casello* (cheese-maker) with the milk from his cows which was then turned into parmigiano reggiano; he can spot a decent wheel of it blindfold. While they were in the buying and bartering mood, they selected a large *prosciutto* (cured ham) with juicy pink meat and creamy fat. Like a lot of the locals, the Lolli family have their own electric machine for slicing prosciutto, such is the frequency with which it is consumed.

While the men were busy with all of this, the women got together to make the cappelletti. Under Gemma's watchful eye, her sister-in-law Chiara, Chiara's sister and her sister-in-law and her sister-in-law's friend, and her friend, rolled, stuffed and shaped trays and trays of the cappelletti at lightning speed. Their loud conversation and incessant laughter rang through the house as they worked. When the job was done everyone, men too, flocked to the kitchen to admire the golden plump cappelletti arranged in neat rows on the wooden trays. The women hung up their aprons, dusted the flour from their clothes and faces and beamed with satisfaction.

Then the guests arrived — from London, from New Zealand — and the party was off with a hiss and a roar. The night before the christening we got together with family and newly arrived friends and toasted the first of the season's chestnuts over the open fire. It was a chance to indulge our friends in a little *ospitalitá Italiana*. Typically it turned into a night of riotous revelry with Isanna's brother Paolo on guitar strumming out the English tunes he knew and the Inglesi belting out 'Torna a Sorrento' and other popular melodies.

The chestnuts were roasted in a large metal frypan, pierced with holes in the base which allows the heat to penetrate, and with a long handle to prevent burns when removing it from the fire. They filled the room with a sweet, nutty perfume. We sprinkled them liberally with salt, and that, along with their dryish texture, was the reason, or so we told ourselves the next day, that we all drank so heartily.

Early on the morning of the christening the house was eerily quiet, but one by one we emerged, no one admitting to a hangover, of course! All too soon the house was swarming with friends and family, the godfather Alberto, coming from the Biuso family home in Genova, and the godmother, my great pal Isanna, groomed and at the ready. We began the celebrations at 12.00 noon by snacking on long diagonal slices of fresh peppercorn salami, platters of creamy moist prosciutto, chunks of piquant tongue-tingling parmigiano reggiano, olives, soft bread and Gemma and Chiara's home-pickled vegetables (*giardiniera*). This might sound unexceptional but the *felino* salami my brother-in-law Ferruccio chooses is exquisite. It's tender, not dry or tough, nor pasty, and it reeks of sweet fat and garlic and peppercorns. The parmigiano reggiano bursts into granular piquant explosions on the tongue. It's not too salty, it's not too sharp, it's just perfect. The salami, parmesan and olives fill the house with savoury aromas that whet the appetite. Everyone hoes in; they know when they're onto a good thing.

Then thirty of us took our places around a very long table, the dozen or more children seated together at their own table, and Gemma and the older women served the first of the regional specialties: *salsa verde*, a piquant sauce of capers and parsley, accompanying the boiled meats reserved from the broth which would be served with the cappelletti, and *zampone*, pig's trotters hollowed out and stuffed with a spicy sausage mixture. This last dish sounds revolting, but it's one of those things that taste better than it sounds. If a zampone comes your way, have a gnaw on it.

Next, steaming bowls of Gemma's clear straw-coloured fragrant broth, filled with plump pillows of cappelletti. Little Ilaria was instantly hooked and refused to eat anything but cappelletti for the rest of the day (she begs me to make them to this day).

For the main course: the pig Aleardo had procured, studded with garlic, rosemary and fennel and spit-roasted; and a magnificent salad and buttery potatoes from his garden.

We staggered over to the church about 3.30 pm for the focus of all this festivity. Our priest, Don Vezzosi, had the red carpet out for us. Not only had we brought our first child all the way from New Zealand to be blessed by his very hands in his own church, but we had brought a second one, and this time with friends from around the world as well. We heard the preceding wedding ceremony was a hurried one. Don Vezzosi had other things on his mind that day: the Lolli–Biuso christening.

With the deed done, the endless hugs, kisses and wishes subsiding, we headed home to undo buttons and loosen belts, to make room for a slice of christening cake and a glass or two of the most special white wine, made by Aleardo, from his own home-grown grapes. Oh yes, it was a good move marrying an Italian.

BOLOGNA THE FAT ONE

The region of Emilia-Romagna produces food which is fresh, rich, tasty and homegrown. It is never 'mean' food; an extra pinch of salt, lump of butter or cup of cream is added fearlessly. Food is to be enjoyed. It is home to prosciutto, parmigiano reggiano, fresh homemade pasta, stuffed pastas, unique fresh and cured pork products, and balsamic vinegar to name but a few items. It is the richest food in all of Italy; the region's capital, Bologna, is known as *la grassa*, the fat one.

Bologna is also home to Europe's oldest and perhaps most beautiful university. Built in the eleventh century, it gives rise to the other nickname for the Bolognesi, *i dotti*, the learned ones. The university caused a housing shortage when it was built, but the practical Bolognesi built upper stories attached to the fronts of the existing buildings, their supports forming 35 kilometres of beautiful porticoes which are still in existence today. The upper stories had to be sufficiently high to allow a man on horseback to pass beneath.

Bologna is a fascinating city, rich in art, history and culinary traditions. No serious gourmand should consider a visit to Italy without a stopover in Bologna.

THE RICHES OF EMILIA-ROMAGNA

SERVES 10

Fennel Salad with Shavings of Parmesan Cheese

Gemma's Salsa Verde

Cappelletti in Brodo
or
Pumpkin Tortelli with Chilli Sage Butter

Loin of Pork with Spiced Stuffing
or
Roasted Chicken with Lemon and Rosemary

Aleardo's Potatoes
Charred Red and Yellow Capsicum Salad

Ricotta Almond Tart

This menu, based on butter not olive oil, is the richest in the book and makes use of the superb specialties of the region of Emilia-Romagna. It's the menu of the Christening Feast we had for Ilaria in 1992 at Reggio Emilia, a city in Emilia-Romagna, situated equidistant between Parma and Modena (slightly northwest of Bologna). The whole menu will serve around ten hungry people, but you can prune back on some of the dishes — and it will still serve ten! I've tried to balance the menu by starting with a light FENNEL SALAD to help digestion; but this can be omitted. The menu will then have one of the pasta dishes as a starter. Alternatively, omit the pasta course and use the fennel salad as a light starter. Fennel bulb must be very fresh to use in a salad; it should be crisp to bite. If the outer parts have dried and shrivelled, discard them and use the crisp inside only (you will therefore need to buy 4–6 bulbs of fennel to make this salad; it's false economy to buy cheaper, less-than-fresh fennel.) The crisp anise-flavoured fennel and piquant parmesan cheese are given a bit of a kick from balsamic vinegar and make an intriguing match, which is at first aromatic, then both slightly sweet and sharp.

Now, a special note about the CAPPELLETTI. This is definitely not the sort of thing you can whip up at short notice, but it is a dish that is very rewarding, and it won't cause you any stress, providing you allow plenty of time for it. It's a traditional stuffed pasta dish, a specialty of the province of Emilia-Romagna; Gemma showed me how to make her version of cappelletti, from Reggio Emilia, many years ago.

You start by making a light, golden broth, infused with vegetables and herbs. Italian broth is much lighter than French stock. Once the broth is seasoned with salt it should be so flavoursome and have such a clear, golden hue that the prospect of consuming a cup full of it, as a kind of 'restorative' broth, is something to salivate over. Once the broth is made, it needs to be refrigerated until any fat sets on the top; this is easily skimmed away. The broth should be made at least a day in advance, and can be frozen.

Making the filling for the cappelletti is the perfect job for a chilly autumn day. The cappelletti can also be frozen: on the day of the feast, they are taken from the freezer about 30 minutes before you cook them, and the broth is thawed and heated. Preparing the broth and cappelletti in advance, as described, means it is possible for one cook to turn out this feast (in Italy there would be several females in the production-line).

Legend has it that *tortellini*, small shaped rings of stuffed pasta similar to cappelletti, were invented in Castelfranco by a peeping-tom innkeeper who saw the navel of Venus when he peeped through the keyhole of her door. He fell in love with Venus, raced off to the kitchen and invented tortellini in her honour. Ah, the romance of these Italian tales. If someone peeped through your keyhole these days, they would probably get arrested.

So, what is the difference between cappelletti and tortellini? When making cappelletti, the pasta is cut into small squares, a knob of filling is put on then the pasta is folded diagonally and shaped around the fingers. The sealed pointed edges of the pasta stick up like a peaked cap, hence the name 'little hat'. In Bologna, they cut the pasta into rounds, put on a knob of filling, fold them in half, shape them around the fingers and fold down the edges.

If this is all in the 'too-hard' basket, then consider the PUMPKIN TORTELLI. These little pillows of sweet pumpkin afloat in a pool of sizzled butter laced with sage and fired with chilli and garlic are easier to make than the cappelletti and exquisite — though it's rather too easy to pig out on them then not be able to budge from the table. It's not traditional, but try them some other time as a winter main course followed by salad. Alternatively, in this menu serve *rigatoni* with Isanna's *porcini ragù* (page 150), increasing the pasta quantity to 700 g (you'll need a large pot to cook it in) and using all the sauce in the recipe.

The PORK LOIN makes excellent eating with its mildly spicy savoury stuffing, moist tender meat and crunchy crackling. I'm often asked how to get good crackling on pork. It's easy. Cook the loin in a shallow-sided dish because high sides on a roasting dish block out direct heat and prevent the fat on the sides of the joint from getting hot enough to crackle (or they trap in steam and soften the crackling). Keep everything off the crackling (don't baste it) apart from a generous coating of oil and salt. Cook it on a very high heat until the fat starts to crackle. Do not cover the crackling once the meat is cooked. If serving the meat cold (it has more flavour served cold), remove the crackling and refrigerate it separately on a plate (don't cover it) until it is cold, then transfer it to a covered container. Serve it within 24 hours. The loin may be prepared several hours ahead — bring back to room temperature before baking. If pork is not to your taste, try the simple-to-prepare chicken dish. Both the tortelli and pork are flavoured with sage — you may prefer to avoid this double up of herbal flavourings.

Use waxy salad potatoes for Aleardo's novel way with POTATOES. Leaving the skin on the potatoes during cooking provides more flavour, conserves nutrients and helps prevent the potatoes becoming waterlogged. However, in this menu, you may find it more convenient to peel them before cooking, rather than having to deal with the proverbial 'hot potato' when you are finishing off the food. Here's a simple test to tell whether the potatoes you have are waxy or floury (waxy ones hold together well after cooking, so are good for salads and sliced dishes; floury ones collapse, making great purées, jacket and roast potatoes). Make a brine with 1 part salt to 11 parts water. Drop in a potato. If it floats, it's waxy; if it sinks, it's floury; and if it hangs around the middle . . . it's anyone's guess!

The roasted RED AND YELLOW CAPSICUM SALAD is the sort of thing which works equally well served as a summery antipasto dish (it will serve 6–8 as an antipasto dish), but I like to include it in this menu for its pretty colours. The sweet capsicum flavours are balanced by the bite of capers.

I've included SALSA VERDE, even though it's not part of this menu. It's a pungent, verdant sauce, made with parsley, capers, garlic, vinegar, mustard and oil. Some versions include chopped hardboiled eggs, breadcrumbs and anchovies. The sauce is often served with *bollito misto*, a selection of meat cuts simmered in a flavoursome broth, which is how I first encountered it at the home of the Lolli family. Gemma always serves it with the meat she has used to make the broth for the cappelletti. It has plenty of other uses, as a dip for crisp vegetables and as a spread on crostini for example, and although not traditional, I find it delicious with hardboiled eggs and smoked fish. If made without eggs it keeps several days, providing it is well covered with olive oil, then covered and refrigerated.

Dessert is an easily prepared RICOTTA TART flavoured with honey and orange rind and studded with roast almonds. It's very easy to squeeze in a tiny sliver of it at the end of the meal with a steaming cup of short black espresso.

FENNEL SALAD WITH SHAVINGS OF PARMESAN CHEESE

SERVES 10

1 buttercrunch or cos lettuce
small wedge fresh parmesan cheese
3 large bulbs fennel
1¹/₂ tablespoons balsamic vinegar
³/₄ teaspoon salt
freshly ground black pepper to taste
120 ml extra virgin olive oil

Wash and dry the lettuce, place it in a plastic bag and refrigerate.

Shave the parmesan cheese into thin curls with a potato peeler, letting the pieces drop gently onto a plate. Cover with an upturned bowl (this is to prevent squashing the curls of cheese; they're delicate). The cheese can be prepared 2–3 hours before required; if the weather is cool, it can be left at room temperature; in hot weather, refrigerate it.

Prepare the fennel by trimming away the root end and removing any bruised parts. Save the feathery leaves and chop coarsely; set aside for the garnish. Cut the bulbs into quarters, slice out the cores and discard, wash well then shake dry. This can be done several hours in advance; transfer the fennel to a plastic bag and refrigerate. About three hours before serving, cut the fennel into wafer-thin slices. Put in a salad bowl, cover and refrigerate. Tear the lettuce into bite-size pieces and add to the bowl.

In a small bowl, blend the balsamic vinegar, salt, black pepper and oil together. Pour over the salad and toss lightly. Arrange the salad on individual plates. Top with the curls of parmesan cheese, garnish with a little chopped feathery fennel and serve immediately.

If preferred, the cheese may be shaved directly over each plate of salad at serving time.

GEMMA'S SALSA VERDE

1¹/₂ cups freshly ground fine white breadcrumbs
2 tablespoons white wine vinegar
2 cups tightly packed, destalked parsley
³/₄ cup salted capers, soaked 10 minutes in warm water then drained (or use capers in brine)
¹/₄ teaspoon salt
2 cloves garlic, roughly chopped
1 teaspoon Dijon-style mustard
¹/₂ cup extra virgin olive oil, or as required

Put the breadcrumbs in a bowl and pour over the vinegar. Leave to soak for 10 minutes.

Put the parsley in the food processor bowl and process until finely chopped, then add to the bowl of breadcrumbs. Next, lightly process the capers, salt, garlic, mustard and oil (don't process to a paste — leave the mixture coarse), then add to the bowl. Blend together, adding more oil if necessary. Cover with plastic wrap and chill until required.

SERVES 10

broth (recipe follows)
cappelletti stuffing (recipe follows)

fresh pasta
600 g flour
6 large free-range eggs
1 teaspoon salt

Make the pasta in two batches in a food processor. Put 3 eggs and half a teaspoon of salt into the food processor bowl. Blend for 5 seconds. Stop the machine and sprinkle on 300 g flour. Blend the mixture together, using the pulse button (15–20 one-second pulses) until the mixture forms tiny beads; do not overwork it or the pasta will be tough. Turn it out onto a dry work surface and press together into a ball. Cover tightly with plastic wrap. Wash and dry the food processor bowl and blade and repeat the procedure with the remaining ingredients. Rest the dough 10–15 minutes before rolling.

Rolling the dough
This is best done with a hand-cranked pasta-rolling machine. Cut one of the balls of dough in half; rewrap half tightly in plastic wrap. Lightly dust the other half of the dough with flour then press it out to approximately 10 cm wide by 15 cm long. Set the blades on the pasta machine at their widest setting (usually no. 1) and feed the pasta through.

Cappelletti in Brodo

Fold the dough in three and repeat the rolling and folding four more times, dusting with flour to prevent sticking. The dough should now be quite smooth, although possibly a little ragged at the edges. Move the rollers to no. 2 setting and roll it through once, then roll it through once on no. 3 setting. Cut the piece of dough in half. Lay one half of the dough on a lightly floured board and cover with a clean dry cloth.

Roll out the other piece of dough once on no. 4 setting and once on no. 5 setting. Flour the sheet of pasta, cut it in half and cover one piece with the clean dry cloth. Roll the other piece of dough once on no. 6 setting then lay it on a lightly floured board. It's now ready to stuff and shape.

(Once you have completed the cappelletti with this dough, take the piece of dough you rolled to no. 5 setting and roll it once on no. 6 setting, stuff it and shape it, then go back to the piece of dough you rolled as far as no. 3 setting and repeat the rolling, cutting, rolling, stuffing and shaping as described.)

Stuffing and shaping the cappelletti
Use a large, clean ruler to cut the pasta into long, even strips, 35–40 cm long by 4 cm wide, then use the ruler to cut the strips into 4 cm squares. Put a very small amount of stuffing in the centre of each square (less than a quarter of a teaspoonful). Fold the square in half diagonally, forming a triangle, and press the edges together (if they will not stick, dab with a little water). Pick up the triangle of pasta with your thumb and index finger and curl it around your index finger, with the pointed parts facing the tip of your finger. Seal the two ends together, forming it into a ring. Next, gently curl the pointed part over so it points towards your hand. And that's it!

Put the cappelletti on a clean, dry cloth, which should be liberally dusted with flour, as they are done. The cappelletti are usually left to air-dry (for up to a week in a cool dry climate) but must be turned often to prevent sticking (obviously they can't be kept so long in humid or warm conditions). I have always found this a hit and miss affair. If the weather is too humid, no matter how many times you turn them, they stick. I prefer to partially air-dry them for 4–5 hours, then cook them; or to freeze them. Freeze on trays (slip trays underneath the cloths), then when the cappelletti are frozen, move them to plastic bags and tie securely.

Remove them from the freezer about 30 minutes before you need them. Lay them on a clean cloth (not touching each other) in a dry place (not a steamy kitchen).

Bring the prepared broth to the boil. Allow 200 ml of broth and 20–24 cappelletti per person. Drop them into the broth, one by one, stirring gently. Bring the broth to the boil then cook, uncovered, at a gentle boil, until the cappelletti are just cooked (al dente). This will take between 5 and 12 minutes, depending on how dry they are.

When they are ready, ladle into heated soup or pasta bowls, with the broth, and serve immediately with freshly grated parmesan cheese.

Although it is not traditional, I prefer to cook the cappelletti in water, not in the broth, so any flour coating washes off in the water rather than in the broth (flour makes the broth lose its clarity). I then dish the hot broth into the bowls and add the drained cappelletti.

Broth for Cappelletti

2 pieces of veal or beef shin (osso buco) approximately 2 cm thick, rinsed
2 extra pieces of bone from the shin, approximately 2 cm thick, rinsed
1 raw chicken carcass and 2–3 wings, or equivalent
uncooked chicken meat and bones, rinsed
1 onion, peeled and quartered
2 carrots, quartered
2 sticks celery, cut into chunks
2 bay leaves
few parsley stalks and sprigs thyme
1 chicken stock cube
salt

Put all the ingredients except the salt in a very large saucepan and cover with cold water. (The pot should be one third full of bones and vegetables and two thirds full of water). Bring to the boil slowly, skimming well. Partially cover with a lid and lower the heat. Cook the stock at a gentle simmer for 2$1/2$ hours. Strain through a colander into a large bowl or saucepan, conserving the strained items, season generously with salt (it should taste delicious), then cool quickly. Cover and refrigerate overnight.

Thoroughly remove the fat from the top (it should be totally defatted). Use as directed. If not for immediate use, the stock can be kept for several days, providing it is brought to the boil once a day, cooled quickly then refrigerated again. Alternatively, freeze it.

Stuffing

1 tablespoon butter
15 ml (1 tablespoon) olive oil
200 g minced beef or veal
200 g minced pork
pinch of ground cloves
$1/2$ teaspoon ground cinnamon
$1/4$ teaspoon grated nutmeg
1 teaspoon salt and freshly ground black pepper to taste
2 large eggs, lightly beaten
1 cup soft fresh breadcrumbs
200 g freshly grated parmesan cheese
vegetables reserved from the broth

Put the butter and oil in a large frypan and set over a high heat. Add the minced meats and break them up with a fork until they lose the raw look. Continue cooking, stirring often, evaporating any liquid. Turn off heat. Tilt pan and leave 5 minutes then transfer to a food processor using a slotted spoon. Add the spices, salt, pepper and eggs. Process until mixed. Transfer to a bowl. Blend in the crumbs and parmesan. Without washing the processor bowl, add the vegetables reserved from the broth. Process to a purée and add enough to the stuffing to make it soft and moist, but not wet. The stuffing can be made a day in advance (cover when cool and refrigerate). Freeze left overs, and use in *ravioli*.

SERVES 6 (makes about 100); double this recipe for the full menu to serve 10

FILLING
800 g pumpkin (choose a firm fleshed variety)
75 g (³/₄ cup) freshly grated parmesan cheese
³/₄ cup fresh white breadcrumbs
few grates fresh nutmeg
¹/₄ teaspoon salt

PASTA
3 eggs, at room temperature
¹/₂ teaspoon salt
300 g flour

SAUCE
50 g fresh butter
²/₃ cup fresh sage leaves
8 tiny dried bird's-eye chillies, crushed
3 large cloves garlic, crushed
extra grated parmesan cheese for serving

To prepare the filling, cut the pumpkin into large chunks, remove the seeds, and put it in a metal colander or steaming basket. Set it over a saucepan of water, cover with a lid and steam 15–20 minutes or until tender. Leave to cool. Scoop the flesh from the skin and place in a bowl. Mash to a purée with a potato masher then mix in the parmesan cheese, crumbs, nutmeg and salt. The filling can be made a day ahead; cover and refrigerate.

Make the pasta according to the instructions on page 75. Lay a long rectangle of rolled pasta, 10 cm wide, on a floured board. Put half-teaspoonfuls of the pumpkin mixture at regular intervals on the dough, 5 cm apart, 2.5 cm in from the edge. Fold the pasta over itself, enclosing the filling; bring the edges to meet. Seal the edges. Cut in between the stuffing with a knife or fluted pastry wheel, forming the tortelli into puffed pillows with one folded edge and three crimped edges. Lay them on trays covered with waxed paper.

Unless I am going to cook the tortelli soon after making, I prefer to freeze them immediately and to cook them from frozen; they are difficult to dry in humid conditions.

When ready to cook, bring a large saucepan of salted water to the boil. Drop the tortelli into the water and cook over a medium heat (rapid boiling will cause them to burst) until the pasta is just tender (4–5 minutes, depending on how dry they are). Lift out with a slotted spoon and drain in a colander. Transfer to bowls for serving.

While the tortelli are cooking, prepare the sauce. Put the butter in a non-stick frypan with the sage, chilli and garlic. Cook gently until the butter is foaming and the garlic is just starting to colour. Take the pan off the heat and immediately pour the contents over the drained tortelli (the sauce only takes 3–4 minutes to cook).

SERVES 10

90 g (1¹/₂ cups) fresh breadcrumbs
90 ml milk
1 onion, very finely chopped
1 tablespoon butter
225 g pork and veal mince (or use pork mince only)
1 tablespoon chopped parsley
2 teaspoons chopped sage
³/₄ teaspoon fennel seeds
¹/₂ teaspoon freshly grated nutmeg
salt and freshly ground black pepper to taste
1 egg, lightly beaten
2 kg boned pork loin (weight after boning), fat scored
olive oil
fresh herbs to garnish

Put the breadcrumbs in a bowl and pour on the milk. Leave to soak 10–12 minutes. Put the onion in a small saucepan with the butter and a tablespoon of water. Cover and cook gently until softened. Cool, then add to the crumbs. Add the minced meat, parsley, sage, fennel seeds, nutmeg, 1 teaspoon of salt and black pepper. Mix well then beat in the egg.

Lay the loin on a board, fat side down. With a sharp knife partially free the nut of meat from the loin without detaching it. Spread some of the stuffing under the nut of meat and over the boned part of the loin. Roll up and tie with string (the stuffing will squelch out; force as much back in as will fit). Cover and refrigerate.

Heat 2 tablespoons of oil in a shallow roasting tin over a medium heat. Rub the fat with oil and sprinkle it generously with salt. When the oil in the roasting tin is hot, place the loin in the tin, fat side up. Bake in an oven preheated to 225°C for 30 minutes (do not baste). When the crackling starts to expand and burst into fat bubbles, lower the heat to 190°C and cook for about 50 minutes more, until the pork is cooked to medium (meat a pale rosy colour, very juicy when pierced with a skewer). Scrape the roasting tin from time to time during cooking to prevent scorching.

Remove the meat from the oven, transfer it to a board and let it rest for 10 minutes. Lift off the crackling, scrape off the uncrackled fat from the underside then cut the crackling into bite-size pieces (easily done with scissors). Put the crackling on a hot serving plate. Remove excess fat from the loin then slice the meat thinly. Arrange on a heated serving plate and garnish with fresh herbs. If liked, skim the fat off the pan juices, pour in a few tablespoons of water, broth or white wine, bubble it up and spoon over the sliced meat.

If there is leftover stuffing, either conserve it for another use or make it into small balls and roast these around the loin (they will cook in about 25 minutes). If there is a small detached piece of meat inside the boned loin (the fillet) the stuffing can be used in this; make a pocket in the meat, put in the stuffing, tie with string and roast separately for about 35 minutes. Alternatively, freeze it for another meal.

Roasted Chicken with Lemon and Rosemary

Serves 8–10

10 chicken thighs
60 ml (4 tablespoons) extra virgin olive oil
30 ml (2 tablespoons) fresh lemon juice
2 teaspoons fresh rosemary sprigs
$^1/_2$ teaspoon salt
freshly ground black pepper to taste
lemon wedges for serving

Trim the chicken of all fat, but leave the skin on. Mix the olive oil, lemon juice, rosemary sprigs, salt and pepper in a shallow dish. Put the chicken joints in the dish and toss gently in the marinade. Leave for about an hour, tossing often.

Heat a large heavy-based frypan over a medium heat. When the pan is hot, drop in enough chicken joints to fit the pan without overcrowding (probably a little more than half); you won't need any extra oil. Brown well to a deep golden, about 10 minutes, adding extra chicken joints as the first batch are done. Transfer them to a shallow-sided ovenproof dish, arranging them in one layer. Pour over the rest of the marinade then transfer to an oven preheated to 180°C and cook for 40 minutes, basting twice.

Serve hot with lemon wedges.

Aleardo's Potatoes

Serves 10

2 kg medium-size waxy salad potatoes
60 g butter
3 cloves garlic, thinly sliced
freshly ground black pepper and salt to taste
2 tablespoons roughly chopped parsley
juice of 1 lemon, strained

Scrub the potatoes then either steam or boil them until tender. As soon as they are cool enough to handle, peel off the skins and slice into thick rounds, keeping the slices together.

Put the butter in a large frying pan. Set over a medium heat and add the garlic when the butter has just melted. Transfer the potatoes to the pan, keeping them in neat mounds of slices, grind on some pepper and sprinkle well with salt. Cook gently until the potatoes are imbued with the flavours of the butter and garlic (about 10 minutes), tossing carefully and spooning the garlic butter over them. Don't let the potatoes and garlic fry.

Sprinkle over the parsley and toss carefully. Turn onto a heated serving platter or into a dish. Pour over the lemon juice and serve immediately.

SERVES 10

3 large red and 3 large yellow capsicums
1 large tomato, peeled
1 clove garlic, crushed
several leaves fresh basil, chopped, or ¹/₄ cup tiny basil leaves
1 tablespoon capers, drained (chop if large)
¹/₄ teaspoon salt and freshly ground black pepper to taste
50 ml extra virgin olive oil
1 tablespoon red wine vinegar

Heat the oven to 200°C. Put the capsicums on the middle rack and place a piece of foil on the rack below to catch any drips. Roast the capsicums for 20–30 minutes, or until barely charred, turning occasionally with tongs. Transfer to a plate and when cool peel off the blackened skins, slip out the cores and seeds and cut each pepper into several pieces; reserve any juices. Arrange in a shallow serving dish. Cut the tomato in quarters and flick out the seeds. Cut into thin strips, discarding the core, and put in a bowl. Add garlic, basil, capers, black pepper, salt, oil and vinegar and capsicum juices. Mix together then spoon over the roasted capsicums. Leave at room temperature for 30 minutes before serving.

RICOTTA ALMOND TART

SERVES 8–10 (best served at room temperature)

125 g whole unblanched almonds
butter
³/₄ cup brioche crumbs, or substitute fresh white breadcrumbs
3 eggs, lightly beaten
300 g ricotta
grated rind of half an orange
³/₄ cup runny honey (choose a mild-flavoured honey)

Preheat oven to 180°C. Put the almonds in a shallow ovenproof dish and bake about 10 minutes, or until browned. Chop roughly, then cool. Butter a 20 cm round spring-form cake tin. Put in the crumbs, and shake to coat the sides, letting the rest settle evenly.

Put the eggs in a bowl, beat lightly with a fork, then mix in the ricotta. Add the orange rind, honey and almonds. Stir together, then tip into tin. Bake in oven preheated to 180°C for about 30 minutes, or until lightly browned, firmish in the centre and just starting to pull away from the sides of the tin. Remove from the oven and cool in the tin. Loosen the tart then remove the side of the tin. Use a palette knife to free the tart from the base, then slide it onto a serving plate. Dust with icing sugar and serve with dollops of whipped cream. It can be prepared several hours before serving.

SUMMERTIME LUNCH UNDER THE PINES

PICNIC

In summertime, my Italian family retreat to their old family villa, 'Querciolo', in the province of Grosseto, Southern Tuscany. It's always chaotic but the chaos is part of the fun.

In the scorching heat of late July you could fry an egg on the courtyard tiles. The shade on the grapevine-covered terrace is where we all cluster, baying for a breath of wind.

We feast, we drink, we fitfully doze away the sweltering afternoons. As the sun starts to sink in the sky, the best part of the day is upon us. Bathed in golden Tuscan sunlight we gather to spin yarns to each other, to revel in each other's company. We wet our beaks with a sip of chilled wine and watch the sun explode into a glorious sunset.

Out of the blue, as if it's a wholly original idea, someone suggests: 'Tomorrow, if it's hot enough to fry an egg on the tiles, let's have lunch under the pines'. Sweaty brows nod in agreement.

This drastically changes the movement in the kitchen in the morning. The rooster will have only just hopped off his perch on the bit of roof directly above my head and stopped his skull-splitting cockadoodling, when I will lazily, hazily, become aware of to-ing and fro-ing. Someone is collecting eggs from the henhouse. Someone else is harvesting salad greens and tomatoes before the sun wilts and shrivels them. I hear the clanking of bottles. Wine and water are carried to the well and put in to chill.

In the kitchen, frittatas are made and stuffed warm between great chunks of crusty bread; rosy-pink veal cutlets are crumbed and fried in hot spitting oil, seasoned with a smidgin of salt and pepper and wrapped when cool with wedges of lemon and sprigs of parsley; salami, parmesan and prosciutto are cut and wrapped in waxed paper and the fruit, bursting with sweet summer juice, is washed.

Then, like sardines in a can, we squeeze into hot cars which no amount of air-conditioning can keep cool, for the ten-minute ride to the coast. The family treat it like a trek up Everest. We have every possible thing we might need.

You smell the pines before you see them, as the already hot morning sun melts their sticky resin. It takes half an hour to find a park — usually in the spot we saw first and rejected. Another half hour is frittered away unloading and searching for, mooting and agreeing on a spot to picnic. The kids are fractious. They go and plunge into the big blue tepid bath of the Mediterranean.

Top: Caponata. Bottom: Mamma Rosa's Potato Frittata;
Artichoke Frittata; Frittata of Barbecued Vegetables

At last we're settled. The rugs, the beach towels, the sandfly repellent, the food and the wine. It's blissfully cool under the umbrella of the pines. The perfume is intoxicating, heady. We graze, we imbibe. We dote on the children. The Italians smoke. They are happy. Their eyes are shining.

Then we seriously eat — about half a kilo of bread per person (some of my family are sylph-like; I don't know where the food goes). We loll and roll about, satiated, undo buttons, strip off. If we are lucky there is twenty minutes' silence, some snoring. Then the exchange of words begins again, women's voices, soft and hushed, incoherent at first, which too quickly reach their crescendo.

This is 'picnic' Italian style. It's not much different to having lunch at home, except the freedom that eating outdoors brings (you know what I mean, the women can't hurry off to their chores in the kitchen), ensures that all family members relax. And the focus of the menu changes too, away from steaming bowls of pasta, rice or soup, which are still served throughout the hot months, to salads and lighter fare accompanied by stacks of bread.

I'm not going to fill this chapter with tales of great Italian picnics I have had; instead I'm going to cram it full of recipes, many of which did not find a natural home in any of the other menus, but which are too good to leave out of this book. To create a picnic menu, choose, say, a frittata, one or two salads, and a tart, *muffuletta* or eggs. If a barbecue, or an oven, is at hand, you can add either the *bruschetta* or the prosciutto wrapped in vine leaves. But first some notes on eggplant.

Eggplant (*melanzane*)

Most eggplant recipes recommend that you sprinkle the sliced or chopped eggplant with salt before cooking to draw out bitter juices. It's worth doing if the eggplant is bitter, but a waste of time if it is not. The question is, how do you tell if an eggplant is bitter?

In my experience, immature eggplants which are heavy for their size, and those tinged with a fair amount of green underneath the skin (visible when you cut or slice them) will be bitter. There is sometimes a detectable smell of unripeness or greenness too, similar to the smell when you cut open a heavy firm unripe green capsicum. Also, eggplants which are full of seeds can be bitter.

If you've ever eaten a bitter eggplant, you'll know how unpleasant it is. If in doubt, salting is a wise precaution.

However, moisture, which is a result of salting, is the enemy of hot oil — it causes spitting and lowers the overall temperature of the oil — and eggplants fry better if they haven't been salted. Yep, salt is the eggplant's Catch-22.

Another point which tends to throw even good cooks into a tailspin is, how much oil to use when frying eggplants? The hot tip is: the hotter the oil, the less of it the eggplant will absorb. Try for yourself. Put a few slices of eggplant into a moderately hot pan over a medium heat with three tablespoons of oil and watch the eggplant suck up the oil like a thirsty sponge. But fry the slices in 'boiling oil', as the Italians do, and you'll be astounded by the difference.

Italians are not timid about using the frying pan and, if a vegetable tastes better fried in oil rather than boiled in water, that's the treatment it will get.

I credit the Sicilians for teaching me how to cook eggplants. Sicily's climate produces superb eggplants, and I reckon they've got it sussed. The eggplants are not salted before they are cooked. They are sliced, air-dried briefly, then lowered into oil that's so hot it's shimmering and on the point of smoking. The oil bubbles around the eggplant slices, quickly cooking them. They emerge a burnished golden brown with crisp taut skin and creamy interior. Most of the oil remains in the pan. The thing you mustn't fear is the temperature of the oil — there has to be a good quantity of it and it has to be HOT.

I think cooks resist frying eggplants in lots of oil because they're convinced that all that oil is bad for one's health. Nothing could be further from the truth — the more oil you use, provided it is shimmering hot, the less of it you'll eventually consume.

I mention elsewhere in the book that Italians don't like to waste anything. The thick absorbent brown paper wrapped around bread and other foodstuffs in Italy is the best blotting paper for draining food I know of. Don't spread the paper out flat; crumple it up and make it crinkly. The food then balances on top of the crinkles and oil drips off and is absorbed by the paper; if fried food sits on flat oily paper the oil absorbed by the paper seeps back into the food. Logical when you think about it.

I have to buck tradition when it comes to choosing a vessel in which to cook the eggplants. I have found that the most successful thing is a wok. The oil can't spread out over a great surface, as it does in a pan — the wok confines it. Because there is a good depth of oil, it maintains a high temperature longer. It's not possible to fry more than 2–3 large slices at a time in a wok, so the oil temperature is not constantly being lowered by too much cold food going in. After use, the oil can be cooled, strained, bottled, stored in a cool dark place and used again.

Another successful method, particularly useful when the eggplant is to be incorporated into a pie or layered dish, is to oven-bake them. Brush the slices on both sides with oil and spread them on a baking tray. Bake for about 30 minutes until golden brown. This method uses the least amount of oil, but it is not a traditional way of dealing with eggplants. If you want to make the recipes 100 per cent authentic, fry the eggplant.

The worst sin you can commit with an eggplant is to serve it 'half raw' — saturated with oil, soggy, and raw in the centre. The astringency makes your mouth contract, and the furry feeling lasts for ages.

Some of the recipes in this book have instructions to salt the eggplant, and some do not. In some recipes I've suggested dry-baking them, to help cut down on the amount of oil in a dish, and subsequent richness.

It's taken me 20 years, and probably 2000 kg of eggplant, to work all this out — silly, really, when all I needed to do was watch how Italians prepare it, then get over my prejudice about the quantity of oil they were using.

SUMMERTIME LUNCH UNDER THE PINES

SERVES 6

Bruschetta with Chickpea Pâté and Barbecued Tomatoes
Bocconcini Wrapped in Prosciutto and Vine Leaves

Isanna's Free-range Eggs

Muffuletta

Salami Tart
Roasted Red Capsicum and Olive Tart
Zucchini and Oregano Tart

Frittata of Barbecued Vegetables
Artichoke Frittata
Mamma Rosa's Potato Frittata
Spinach Frittata

Roasted Yellow Capsicum and Mozzarella Salad
Caponata
Baked Eggplants with Capers and Tomatoes
Warm Green Bean and Red Onion Salad
Charred Zucchini with Pesto

Rich Shortcrust Pastry

Iced Coffee

From top right: Roasted Yellow Capsicum and Mozzarella Salad; Roasted
Red Capsicum and Olive Tart; Zucchini and Oregano Tart

One of the most appealing aspects of Italian cookery is its simplicity. ISANNA'S FREE-RANGE EGGS is a good example. The dish requires few special ingredients and takes no more than five minutes to make, but it tastes sensational. Make it with the first of the season's mild garlic.

To prevent the egg shells from cracking during cooking, use the point of a dressmaking pin to prick the rounded end of each egg, where there is a small air-sac. The pinhole acts as an escape valve; as the contents of the egg swell during cooking, this forces the air out of the air-sac, preventing the shells from cracking. Having the eggs at room temperature and bringing them slowly to the boil also helps. To stop a grey ring forming around the yolk after cooking, cool the eggs quickly by running plenty of cold tap water over them.

The BRUSCHETTA is a modern adaptation of a rustic treatment for bread. The sweet tomatoes set against the mealy taste of chickpeas, biting zing of garlic and fresh flavours of mint, make this a delectable nibble. Mint is not often used in Italian cooking, but I like the freshness it provides in this recipe.

You'll get a crisper base to the pastry for the TARTS if you use a flan ring, rather than a dish. A flan ring placed on a baking tray produces a crisper base because any moisture can freely run out from underneath the flan ring and evaporate. In a flan dish, the moisture is trapped in the dish underneath the pastry, and it can cause the pastry to become soggy. The heat can penetrate the pastry more effectively through a thin metal tray as opposed to a chunky china or glass flan dish.

The pastry cases for the three tarts are 'baked blind' before the filling goes in. This is a term which means the pastry is partially cooked, until it can support itself. It's very useful when the filling is a moist one, and particularly helpful if the oven you are using doesn't brown things well on the bottom. If the filling is already cooked and only requires to be heated in the oven, or if the filling is left uncooked, for example in a fresh fruit tart, the pastry is cooked entirely by this method.

Beans are used to support the pastry until it is cooked or set in position. Don't waste money on expensive metal pastry weights as you can use inexpensive ingredients such as pasta, rice, dried peas or dried beans. They can be used many times; when they get smelly, replace them.

Paper is used to make the removal of them easier and to prevent the beans from becoming embedded in the pastry. Tissue paper is soft and if well crinkled, it can mold easily into any shape. It remains soft after baking and can be lifted out without disturbing the pastry. Both greaseproof paper and aluminium foil can tear the pastry if they are used.

For all the tarts, the pastry can be made a day in advance and lined into the flan ring; keep it in the refrigerator until ready to cook it (or freeze it, then remove the flan ring). Pastry is best eaten the day it is cooked. The ROASTED RED CAPSICUM AND OLIVE TART is exquisite but it requires quite a lot of preparation (much of which can be done in advance). The easiest tart to make is the SALAMI TART.

Knowing how to make a FRITTATA, a flattish Italian egg dish, can get you out of many a mealtime crisis. In no time at all, and with few ingredients, you can have a nutritious, tasty dish. The trick lies in using a well-oiled pan, cooking the vegetables first and not making the frittata too thick.

MAMMA ROSA'S POTATO FRITTATA is legendary. You can get away with using less oil —

but this is how much she used. If the oil is hot enough, it gives the frittata a crisp lacy edge which tastes delicious.

The ARTICHOKE FRITTATA is wonderfully nutty and good hot or cold. Use well-trimmed, young artichokes for this, or cheat and use Italian artichokes in olive oil. The spinach frittata is a light and tasty recipe from Isanna which is easily put together for a simple family meal. Have you ever wondered what to do with leftover BARBECUED VEGETABLES? Here's the answer — mix them with a few eggs and some grated parmesan cheese and turn them into this little stunner.

There are three different ways of cooking the second side of the frittata. The easiest way is to cook it still in the pan, under the grill. This is not my favoured method because it is easy to make the frittata dry.

If the pan is not too heavy or cumbersome, you can lay a large plate on top of the pan, flip the pan, lift it off and slide the frittata back into the pan to cook the second side.

If the pan is too heavy and hot, slide the frittata out onto a plate, cover the frittata with another plate, flip, then slide the frittata back into the pan.

CAPONATA. Now here's a dish to talk about. Originating in Sicily, caponata in various forms has spread throughout much of Italy. Essentially it is a stew of eggplant, onion and celery, sharpened with vinegar, capers and olives. But there is much more to it than that. A baroque rendition sees the dish adorned with baby octopus and bitter chocolate and toasted almonds added to the sauce. I favour Mamma Rosa's version. But I confess, I've never made it as good as she did. I saw her make it heaps of times and each time I made some mental adjustment which I was sure would help me perfect it. Remo used to grunt 'it's okay' when I first offered it to him, and I have progressed to a 'not bad', but he's never got carried away and said 'nearly as good as Mamma's', or, as he has for my gnocchi, 'better than Mamma's' (actually, moment of truth, I found out years later that she NEVER made gnocchi!). So I reckon it must have been the bowl she served it in which made it so good — the same one she used for her *arancini*!

Anyway, the good thing is, you haven't got Mamma Rosa's bowl of caponata sitting in front of you to compare it to, so chances are you'll be more than delighted with this recipe.

The ROASTED YELLOW CAPSICUM SALAD works well as a salad starter to a summery meal. The other salads in here are all tasty and worth a try, and can be used as antipasti dishes, or as salads and picnic dishes.

Iced coffee is incredibly invigorating on a hot summer's day, especially if you are feeling lethargic. Make good strong coffee from freshly ground or vacuum-packed Italian roast coffee, and add sugar to sweeten. Make the coffee stronger and sweeter than you normally make it for drinking.

Try it with crushed ice or poured over ice cubes. It's also delicious poured over ice cream, topped with a swirl of cream and served as a light dessert. For a change, add a strip or two of lemon peel or a couple of sprigs of mint to the coffee as it is cooling. Also try flavouring the coffee with honey, cinnamon and nutmeg. Put a tablespoon of runny honey in each glass, add some shaved ice and pour over the coffee.

SERVES 6

300 g can chickpeas, drained and rinsed
salt
2 tablespoons lemon juice, strained
1 clove garlic, crushed
freshly ground black pepper to taste
extra virgin olive oil
1 tablespoon finely chopped parsley
1 tablespoon finely chopped mint, plus sprigs for garnishing
6 firm plum or outdoor tomatoes, halved
castor sugar
1 loaf ciabatta bread, sliced, (or use French bread)
1 large clove garlic

Put the chickpeas in a food processor with ¼ teaspoon salt, the lemon juice, garlic, black pepper and 1 tablespoon of extra virgin olive oil. Add 1 tablespoon of water and process until smooth, adding an extra tablespoon of water if the mixture is too thick. Transfer to a bowl and blend in the parsley and mint. Cover and chill until required (this can be made up to a day in advance); bring to room temperature before serving.

When ready to prepare the bruschetta, cook the tomatoes first, then the bread. Oil the tomatoes, sprinkle the cut side with salt then dust with castor sugar. Cook on a heated barbecue grill, cut side down, until lightly browned. Turn and quickly cook the second side then transfer to a plate.

Toast the slices of bread over the heated barbecue grill (watch the heat is not too high or the bread will burn). Transfer to a board, rub each slice with the cut clove of garlic, drizzle on a little extra virgin olive oil and sprinkle with salt. Spread the chickpea pâté on the grilled bruschetta and top each slice with a roasted tomato and a leaf of mint. Serve immediately.

BOCCONCINI WRAPPED IN PROSCIUTTO AND VINE LEAVES

Wrap drained balls of *bocconcini mozzarella* in prosciutto then in rinsed and blanched preserved vine leaves, or fresh young vine leaves rinsed and blanched. Transfer the bundles to a shallow ovenproof dish, drizzle with extra virgin olive oil and bake for about 10 minutes, or till the cheese melts. Serve immediately with a dollop of homemade tomato sauce with chopped olives and basil, and crusty ciabatta. Alternatively, serve with strips of roasted red capsicum.

ISANNA'S FREE-RANGE EGGS

SERVES 4-6

6 free-range medium eggs, at room temperature
salt
2 tablespoons coarsely chopped parsley
1 tablespoon finely chopped fresh garlic (preferably use new season
garlic; don't use soft or mouldy garlic)
freshly ground black pepper to taste
paprika
small black Ligurian 'olivelle' olives (optional)
extra virgin olive oil

Prick the eggs with a dressmaking pin as described in the menu notes, carefully lower them into a pan of gently boiling water and cook for 7 minutes. Drain off the water, then let the cold tap run over the eggs for 5 minutes to cool them quickly. Shell them carefully (they will be fragile), pat dry, cut in half and arrange on a plate.

Sprinkle the eggs with a little salt, the parsley and garlic. Grind on some black pepper then sieve over a little paprika and garnish with the olives, if you are using them. Drizzle with a little oil and serve immediately with good crusty bread.

Isanna's Free-range Eggs

Muffuletta is the 'sandwich supremo'!

Buy a round loaf of crusted bread, cut a cap off and remove all the soft crumb. Fill with layers of baby salad leaves, chopped sundried or semi-dried tomatoes, stoned black or green olives, prosciutto or ham, sliced bocconcini, peppercorn salami, marinated button mushrooms and sliced cherry tomatoes. Douse with a herby dressing, put the top back on, tie with coarse string or raffia and wrap in tinfoil. Best picnic sandwich ever.

SALAMI TART

SERVES 6

23 cm flan ring or dish lined with rich shortcrust pastry, chilled (see page 101)
2 eggs
pinch of salt
pinch of cayenne pepper
2 tablespoons coarsely chopped parsley
200 ml milk
250 g (about 30 thin slices) salami
100 g bocconcini mozzarella in whey, drained and sliced
3 tablespoons freshly grated parmesan cheese

Preheat oven to 180°C. Prick the bottom and sides of the pastry with a fork then line with a double thickness of crumpled tissue paper. Fill with baking beans or rice and bake blind for 15 minutes. Remove from the oven and lift off the paper and beans or rice. Return the pastry to the oven for five minutes more.

In a bowl lightly beat the eggs together then add the salt, cayenne pepper, parsley and milk. Arrange the sliced salami on the pastry base then cover with the sliced bocconcini. Pour on the egg mixture and sprinkle over the parmesan cheese.

Return to the oven and cook a further 25 minutes, or until the pastry and topping are crisp and golden. Cool 10 minutes before removing the flan ring. Serve hot or warm, cut into slices.

FRESH WHITE BREADCRUMBS

Soft white crumbs are used in stuffings and fillings to absorb liquids and flavours, and to give body and a light texture. They do not stay fresh very long as, like bread, they ferment. They will keep in the refrigerator for several days, or they can be frozen — then there are crumbs to have on hand when time is short (thaw for about 10 minutes at room temperature).

Use a loaf of day-old bread, remove all crusts and blend the soft crumbs in a food processor or blender until smooth. Store in a plastic bag. Fresh white crumbs may be dried.

ROASTED RED CAPSICUM AND OLIVE TART

SERVES 8

25–28 cm flan ring lined with rich shortcrust pastry, chilled (see page 101)
1 egg yolk, lightly beaten
1/2 cup freshly grated parmesan cheese
2 large red capsicums
2 large yellow capsicums
60 ml (4 tablespoons) olive oil
400 g can Italian tomatoes, mashed
2 tablespoons tomato paste
salt
1/4 teaspoon sugar
1/4 teaspoon dried oregano
freshly ground black pepper to taste
3 large red onions, chopped
2 tablespoons chopped basil
1/4 cup fresh white breadcrumbs
16 black olives, stoned

Prick the bottom and sides of the pastry with a fork then line it with a double thickness of crumpled tissue paper. Fill with baking beans or rice and bake blind in an oven preheated to 180°C for 15 minutes. Remove from the oven and lift off the paper and beans or rice. Return the pastry to the oven for 10–12 minutes, or until lightly browned all over. Remove from the oven and immediately brush the bottom and sides of the pastry with the beaten egg. Sprinkle with 2–3 tablespoons of the parmesan cheese and set aside.

Sit the capsicums on an oven rack in an oven preheated to 200°C and roast for about 20 minutes, or until blistered and charred. Transfer to a plate and when cool enough to handle, peel and remove the cores and seeds. Cut the capsicums into thick strips.

Put 1 1/2 tablespoons of the oil in a saucepan and add the tomatoes, tomato paste, a pinch of salt, sugar and oregano and a good grinding of black pepper. Bring to the boil, then lower the heat and cook gently, partially covered, for 20 minutes. Remove lid and cook until thick and pulpy; stir often.

Put the onions in a frying pan with the remaining oil and cook over a gentle heat until soft and lightly golden. Grind on some pepper and mix in the basil.

Spread the onion mixture over the pastry bottom, sprinkle over the breadcrumbs and spoon over the tomato sauce. Arrange the capsicums and olives on top. Sprinkle over the rest of the parmesan cheese and return the pie to the oven for 25 minutes or until golden on top. Serve warm, cut into slices.

ZUCCHINI AND OREGANO TART

SERVES 6

23 cm flan ring lined with rich shortcrust pastry, chilled (see page 101)
650 g yellow or green zucchini, trimmed
knob of butter
1 small onion, finely chopped
¹/₂ teaspoon salt
freshly ground black pepper to taste
2 eggs and 1 egg yolk
200 ml cream
¹/₄ teaspoon dried oregano
¹/₂ cup freshly grated parmesan cheese

Preheat oven to 180°C. Prick the bottom and sides of the pastry with a fork then line it with a double thickness of crumpled tissue paper. Fill with baking beans or rice and bake blind for 15 minutes. Remove from the oven and lift off the paper and beans or rice. Return the pastry to the oven for 10–12 minutes, or until lightly browned all over. Remove it from the oven.

Meanwhile, slice three of the zucchini very thinly on the diagonal and set aside for the top. Slice the rest of the zucchini into thinnish rounds and put them in a large frying pan with the butter and onion. Sprinkle with salt and grind on some pepper. Cook gently until softened, but not browned (about 10 minutes). Cool.

Beat the eggs and egg yolk together with the cream and add the oregano. Tip the cooked zucchini into the pastry case, level the top and arrange the raw zucchini on the top in concentric rings. Pour over the custard, ensuring all the zucchini slices on the top are covered with some of it, then sprinkle on the cheese.

Bake for 15 minutes, or till golden on top. Serve warm, cut into slices.

FRITTATA OF BARBECUED VEGETABLES

SERVES 6

1 teaspoon olive oil
2 cups left-over barbecued vegetables (eggplant, red onion, yellow and
red capsicums, zucchini), diced
$^1/_4$ teaspoon salt
freshly ground black pepper to taste
6 eggs
25 g ($^1/_4$ cup) freshly grated parmesan cheese
$^1/_4$ cup basil leaves, chopped

Put the oil in a large frying pan and set over a medium-high heat. Add the vegetables and cook 2–3 minutes, till heated through. Sprinkle over the salt and grind on some pepper.

Meanwhile, break the eggs into a bowl, beat lightly with a fork, then blend in the cheese and basil. Scoop the vegetables out of the pan with a slotted spoon, transferring them to the egg mixture. Combine lightly with a fork.

Pour the mixture into the hot pan and cook the frittata till golden on the bottom, then set the pan under a hot grill and cook till top is golden. Ensure the frittata is loose on the bottom of the pan, then slide it out onto a large flat plate. Serve at room temperature.

Fennel, artichokes and chillies from the garden

SERVES 6

4 young artichokes
juice of 1 lemon mixed with 2 litres cold water
30 ml (2 tablespoons) olive oil
5 eggs
75 g ($^3/_4$ cup) freshly grated parmesan cheese
freshly ground black pepper to taste
1 tablespoon finely chopped marjoram (or $^1/_2$ teaspoon dried marjoram)

Trim the artichoke stems, then cut off the top third of each and discard. Pull off the tough outside leaves, leaving only the very tender leaves near the centre. Slice the artichokes in half and scrape out any choke (fibrous hairs). Drop into acidulated water as they are done, then shake off any excess water, and cut into wafer-thin slices.

Set a large frying pan over a medium heat and add the olive oil. When it is hot, drop in the artichokes. Sauté for about 15 minutes, stirring often, or until they are a light golden brown colour. Pour in $^1/_2$ cup water, stir with a spoon, then put on the lid and lower the heat. Cook gently for about 30 minutes, or until very tender.

Meanwhile, lightly beat the eggs in a bowl and add the parmesan cheese, black pepper and marjoram. Pour this over the artichokes in the frying pan and cook over a low to medium heat until partially set and golden on the bottom. Loosen the frittata from the pan, then cover the pan with a large plate, flip over, lift off the pan and slide the frittata back into the pan to cook the second side. Cook until golden, then slide onto a serving plate.

Serve at room temperature.

If using prepared artichokes in oil, drain off most of the oil, slice them then heat them in the pan. When hot pour on the egg mixture and cook as described.

SERVES 6

100 ml olive oil
300 g potatoes, peeled and cut into smallish cubes
1 large onion, finely sliced
2–3 cloves garlic, finely chopped
freshly ground black pepper to taste
5 eggs
4 tablespoons freshly grated parmesan cheese
2 tablespoons fresh white breadcrumbs
1 tablespoon finely chopped parsley
1 teaspoon finely chopped marjoram, or $^1/_2$ teaspoon dried marjoram
$^1/_4$ teaspoon salt

Heat the oil in a large frypan over a medium heat. Pat the potato cubes dry with kitchen paper then carefully tip them into the oil. Turn to coat in the oil then cook about 20 minutes, or until lightly golden all over, lowering the heat a little if the potatoes start browning too quickly.

Add the sliced onion and garlic to the pan, grind over some pepper, toss with the potatoes then set the heat to low and cover the pan with a lid. Cook approximately 10 minutes or until the potatoes are tender and the onion soft and translucent.

Meanwhile, break the eggs into a bowl, add the parmesan cheese, breadcrumbs and herbs. Mix lightly with a fork. Remove the lid from the pan, sprinkle over salt and grind on some pepper. Toss again. Tilt the pan and drain the oil to one side. Scoop out the potatoes and onion and transfer to the bowl with the egg mixture. Mix well.

Set the pan back on the element, increase the temperature to medium-high and heat until the oil is hot. Pour in the egg mixture, then lower the heat again and cook slowly until partially set on top and golden on the bottom. Loosen the frittata from the pan then slide out on to a flat plate with the help of a spatula. Cover with another plate, flip over then slide back into the pan, uncooked side facing down, and cook the second side until golden. Slide onto a serving plate. Serve warm or at room temperature.

Spinach Frittata

Serves 4–6

200 g fresh spinach leaves, destalked and washed
5 eggs
$^1/_2$ teaspoon salt
freshly ground black pepper to taste
freshly ground nutmeg to taste
100 g (1 cup) freshly grated parmesan cheese
30 ml (2 tablespoons) extra virgin olive oil

Blanch the spinach leaves in a saucepan of boiling water for 20 seconds. Drain, refresh with cold water, then squeeze out excess water. Chop finely.

Break the eggs into a bowl and beat lightly with a fork. Mix in half a teaspoon of salt, a little pepper and nutmeg, the cheese and spinach.

Preheat the grill. Heat the oil in a non-stick pan (about 23 cm diameter) over a medium heat. When it is hot, pour in the egg mixture. Cook until a good golden brown on the bottom. Cook the top of the frittata under the grill until lightly browned. Loosen from the pan and turn onto a plate. Serve warm or at room temperature.

Roasted Yellow Capsicum and Mozzarella Salad

Serves 6

3 large yellow capsicums
150 g bocconcini mozzarella
$^1/_2$ cup red cherry tomatoes
15 ml (1 tablespoon) red wine vinegar
45 ml (3 tablespoons) extra virgin olive oil
$^1/_2$ teaspoon salt
freshly ground black pepper to taste
1 tablespoon capers, drained
1 tablespoon chopped marjoram

Set the capsicums on an oven rack with tinfoil in a pan below to catch the juices. Cook in an oven preheated to 200°C for about 20 minutes or until blistered and charred. Transfer to a bowl and when cool enough to handle, peel off the blackened skins and discard the cores and seeds. Cut the capsicums into thick strips and set aside, with the juices.

Drain the bocconcini, pat dry with kitchen paper and slice thinly. Arrange the yellow capsicums on a plate with the bocconcini and cherry tomatoes.

Whisk together the red wine vinegar, olive oil, salt, pepper, capers and marjoram in a bowl, and add 1 tablespoon of capsicum juices. Spoon over the salad and serve.

Caponata

Serves 6, or 12 as an entrée

1 kg eggplant (2 very large ones, or 3 medium-large ones), cut into large cubes
1 cup olive oil
10 sticks (about half a head) celery, cut into 2–3 cm lengths
1 large onion, finely sliced
5 tablespoons tomato concentrate
1 tablespoon sugar
$^1/_2$ teasppoon salt
freshly ground black pepper to taste
$^3/_4$ cup good quality red wine vinegar
2 tablespoons capers, drained (use salted capers,
rinsed and soaked in warm water for 30 minutes)
$^1/_2$ cup pimento-stuffed green olives, drained

Cut the eggplant into large cubes. Heat most of the oil in a large deep saucepan over a high heat, until a faint haze is given off, then carefully drop in half the eggplant cubes. Stir to coat them in the oil, lower the heat to medium and fry until they are a light golden brown and about half cooked. Tilt the pan, scoop them out with a slotted spoon and transfer them to a large bowl. Add a little more oil to the pan and repeat the process with the second batch of eggplant cubes.

Add a little more oil to the pan, then fry the celery chunks until lightly browned, stirring often (the celery should be half tender; cook about 12–15 minutes). Transfer the celery to the bowl. Lower the heat and add the onion. Cover with a lid and cook gently until softish and lightly coloured.

Dilute the tomato concentrate with four tablespoons of water and mix in the sugar, salt, black pepper and vinegar. Pour into the pan and mix in the capers, olives, fried eggplant, celery and onion. Bring to a gentle boil, lower the heat and cook gently for 15–30 minutes, partially covered, stirring occasionally, or till tender. Leave to cool and serve at room temperature.

BAKED EGGPLANTS WITH CAPERS AND TOMATOES

SERVES 6

2 large eggplants
salt
4 tablespoons chopped canned Italian tomatoes (flesh only)
60 ml (4 tablespoons) extra virgin olive oil
2 tablespoons capers, drained
2 tablespoons chopped basil
2 large cloves garlic, crushed
freshly ground black pepper to taste
2 tablespoons finely ground breadcrumbs

Cut the eggplants in half lengthwise. Score the surface with a sharp knife, sprinkle with salt, then leave them to drain in a colander. After 40 minutes, squeeze them, pat them dry with kitchen paper, and sit them cut side up in a shallow, oiled baking dish.

In a small bowl blend the tomato flesh, olive oil, capers, basil, garlic and black pepper. Spread over the eggplants, sprinkle on the crumbs, then turn over in the dish so they sit cut side down.

Cook for 30 minutes in an oven preheated to 180°C, then turn them over with a spatula. Cook for a further 15–20 minutes, or until very tender. If the eggplants are not browned, grill them briefly. Cool, then cut into chunks and serve.

WARM GREEN BEAN AND RED ONION SALAD

SERVES 4

400 g green beans, topped and tailed
salt
45 ml (3 tablespoons) extra virgin olive oil
1 medium red onion, sliced into rings
1 small clove garlic, crushed
freshly ground black pepper to taste
15 ml (1 tablespoon) balsamic vinegar

Plunge the beans into a saucepan of salted water and cook until tender. Drain, refresh with cold water then pat them dry with absorbent kitchen paper.

Put the oil in a frying pan, set it over a low heat and add the onion and garlic. Cook gently until the onion is soft (don't let it colour). Sprinkle over a pinch of salt, grind on some pepper and mix in the balsamic vinegar. Add the beans to the pan, toss gently then tip the contents of the pan into a serving dish. Serve warmish.

CHARRED ZUCCHINI WITH PESTO

SERVES 6

6–8 firm smallish zucchini, green or yellow
15 ml (1 tablespoon) extra virgin olive oil
salt
freshly ground black pepper
2 tablespoons pesto, preferably homemade

Trim the zucchini, cut them in half down the length, then score the cut surfaces with a sharp knife. Put them in a large bowl and drizzle with the oil. Sprinkle on a little salt and grind on some pepper then rub the oil and seasonings all over the zucchini.

Cook them on a hot barbecue plate till lightly charred. If the pesto is stiff, thin it with a little warm water. Spread it over the cut surfaces of the zucchini then stack them on a plate. Serve at room temperature.

RICH SHORTCRUST PASTRY

225 g plain flour
pinch of salt
170 g butter, softened and pliable but not oily
1 egg yolk
3–4 tablespoons ice-cold water (chill in freezer)

Sift the flour with a pinch of salt into a large mixing bowl. Cut the butter into large lumps and drop it into the flour. Using two knives, cut the butter through the flour until the pieces of butter are like small marbles. Use your fingertips to rub the butter into the flour until the mixture resembles coarse breadcrumbs.

Mix the egg yolk and water together and add it all at once to the flour mixture (use 3 tablespoons of water to begin with; if the pastry seems a little dry and flaky during mixing, sprinkle the extra water onto the dry flakes). Stir with a knife to combine. Lightly knead with the hands and turn out onto a cool, dry, lightly floured surface. Knead briefly until smooth. Wrap in plastic film and refrigerate for 30 minutes (this is important, as it allows the fat to cool and firm, which will prevent sticking during rolling out, and it relaxes the gluten in the flour, which will help minimise shrinkage).

Roll out thinly, using a smooth rolling pin, with short movements, rolling away from your body. Occasionally flour the rolling pin and the board underneath the pastry to prevent sticking. Don't flour the top of the pastry, as the flour will get rolled in and can make the surface of the pastry dry. Cut and shape as required.

ICED COFFEE

See Menu Notes

Passion for Puglia

A Truly Amazing Feast

If you head south down the coast from Bari, in the region of Puglia, till you come to Monopoli, then take the inland road to Alberobello, you'll find yourself in a unique part of Italy. This we discovered on one of our meandering escapades.

The rugged land here is covered with carob and olive trees and dotted with dwellings called *trulli*, which look like giant beehives. The making of trulli dates back centuries, but most of the dwellings standing today have been erected in recent times. They are made from the calcareous rock which has to be dug out of the ground in order to clear the land for crops. The rocks, which jut inwards to form a dome, are arranged in concentric rings and layered up dry without mortar. You're bound to find a local person willing to show you inside one of these fascinating structures.

The day we were in Alberobello was an important one for the town. A local couple were being married in the church in the main *piazza*. The church bells chimed relentlessly for fifteen minutes; shutters were pulled down, closing shop entrances; and traffic ground to a halt. There was an air of expectancy and we hung around in the square outside the church to watch the events. At last the happy couple emerged from the church, kissed and rejoiced as their guests and the local townsfolk gathered around them and young children broke into spontaneous dancing.

After trying unsuccessfully to tag on to the wedding party (we were sure there was a feast in store somewhere!) we hopped into a restaurant we had spotted earlier, tucked inside a group of trulli dwellings. It was called the Ristorante Trullo d'Oro, and our lunch turned out to be truly amazing. A mouthwatering display of antipasti dishes (dishes to nibble on before the main course) caught my eye, and I exclaimed to a passing waiter in my best Italian, 'Everything looks so good, I'd like to try it all.'

We were seated at our table, pondering the tempting menu choices over a glass of Locorotondo, a local white wine, when suddenly the action hotted up. Holy mackerel! The waiter thought I was serious. Over the next ten minutes, twenty-four antipasti dishes were delivered to our table. Luckily, Remo has a sense of humour, but he warned me, if I ever did anything like this again, he'd walk out and leave me to eat the lot.

The food was served in small chunky pottery bowls, except for the bubbling cheese dishes, which were served in small cast-iron pots. Our table was quite small, but that didn't present a problem for the waiter. He simply stacked up bowls in two or three tiers and left us to it. I bet they laughed themselves silly in the kitchen.

The antipasti, which totally overawed us at first, consisted of the following: charred red and green capsicums and capers in oil; fleshy sundried tomatoes which were salty and quite jammy in flavour; a delicious piece of sweet onion tart with buttery pastry; fried crescent-shaped pastries with a ricotta filling; fat brown beans with strong white onions in vinegar and oil; fried balls of spongy cheese in tomato sauce (these must be eaten hot or the cheese turns peculiar); a couple of chunks of *porchetta* (roasted pork); sweet and sour red onions; bubbling chunks of grilled cheese; roasted bruschetta with oil, herbs and tiny sweet tomatoes; fresh, unsalted anchovies; small marinated artichoke hearts; boiled yellow lupin beans (you flick off the skins — very nutty); fried cauliflower florets in batter; cauliflower and *funghi trifolati* (sautéd in oil with garlic and parsley); fried zucchini in batter; mozzarella dressed with oil and fresh herbs; *scamorza* cheese (similar to mozzarella) with tomatoes, olives and capers (very rich and tasty); fat plump olives; and grilled *straciatella* (a type of cheese). All we needed after that lot was a refreshing salad to cut through the oil slick building up on our palates, and a crane to lift us off our seats and out of the restaurant.

Driving back to our hotel at La Mola, on the coast about ten minutes out of central Bari, we passed a busy fish market where we pulled up for a look. It was 6.00 pm and already dark. The fishing boats had just come in with their catches and the men were unloading the fish onto marble tables. The fish, with bulging eyes and flapping tails, sparkled and glistened in the fluorescent light, giving off that fresh seawater odour which stings the nostrils. Within fifteen minutes of being brought to shore, the fish had been sold, packed into ice and whizzed off to the city's restaurants, where they would feature on the evening's menus as 'fresh fish of the day'. When you order fresh fish in Bari, you can be sure that's what you'll get. The marble tables were hosed down, the floor disinfected and then all that was left for the fisherfolk to do was to sit and smoke and tell lies about 'the one that got away'.

That evening, weighted down by our lunchtime repast, we flagged dinner and instead went for a brisk walk. As we were walking down one of the back streets, there was a commotion going on in one of the fruit shops. We looked in and saw a group of people unpacking crates of grapes. They were the biggest grapes I have ever seen, the size of golf balls! My eyes must have said it all, because the next thing I heard behind me was 'Would Signora like to try the grapes?' and there, standing in the doorway of the run-down shop, was a young signorina with an enormous bunch of grapes for me. They refused any money, and embarrassed, turned and went back to their work. The grapes were *zibibbo*, huge, pale green and smooth-skinned, luscious, sweet and the best grapes I have ever eaten.

Mussels in Tomato Broth

Puglia has huge appeal. It's a land of surprises too. Friendly folk seem to pop out of the woodwork when you least expect them. The food is, in many cases, unusual and different, and more often than not, utterly delicious. It's an uncomplicated cuisine, like that of Tuscany but more intriguing.

The olive trees stretch for miles and miles; but there are mountains, plains and coastline also, which give rise to a curious culinary mix based on the wheat belt, the market garden, sheep and shepherds, the vineyard and the bounty of the sea, and of course the olive grove.

THE TWO GLUTTONS

I once met a real character in the city of Bari. His name was Cleto. He was the export manager of a specialist pasta company, and he had been ordered by his boss to entertain us. Dutifully he showed us the sights of Bari, until he happened to ask us what work we did. Food, we said. He rolled his eyes heavenward, blew a kiss to the sky, then burnt some rubber as he jerked the car into a quick U-turn and headed off in another direction, muttering something about our being better off spending the night eating and drinking. We didn't argue. He took us to a superb restaurant, aptly named 'Due Ghiottoni' (the two gluttons) and there he stuffed us full of Barese specialties.

It was dawn before we farewelled him like an old friend. What food, what stories, and what an eye-opener to this culinary treasure-trove of Italy.

We had been seated in the Due Ghiottoni no more than two minutes when a spicy garlicky aroma signalled the arrival of a platter of coarse salami. Locally made, it was richly flavoured and studded with peppercorns which sneakily burst into fire on the tongue just when you thought it was safe to bite into them, and salty enough to make me gulp down half a glass of Locorotondo. Straciatella, a type of bland milky cheese sitting in whey which separates into thin strands when you pick it up in the fingers, was a good follow-on and helped to extinguish the fire on the tongue. Crunchy potato fritters and *panzarottini*, which are small deep-fried pastries shaped into crescents filled with a savoury ham and cheese mixture, and some more bland milky cheese in the form of small 'bites' of fresh bocconcini mozzarella, followed.

I hadn't heard Cleto order anything, but I'd only just swished the grease-slick off my palate with another slug of Locorotondo, when our jovial waiter delivered Cleto's *pièce de résistance*: a platter of raw seafood. Remo went green around the gills as he watched Cleto suck down a whole baby squid (*calamaretti*) in one go, with nary a chomp or sideways glance. I was counting on him to be brave because I knew I couldn't muster the nerve to try it. Manly pride at stake, Remo followed suit and devoured three of them, followed by raw mussel, oyster and clam chasers, before he knew it. Cleto beamed at him. I merely squirmed in my seat and fiddled around with a small cache of dainty sea *datteri* (local crustacean) and little clams, which were both sweet and delicious with a squirt of refreshing lemon.

Since Cleto worked for a pasta company, I was sure the meal would comprise a pasta course. I was not wrong; I just hadn't anticipated that there would be more than one dish. Steaming plates of *cannerozzetti*, a small ridged tubular pasta arrived, smothered in a sauce of Italian parsley, ripe sweet tomatoes and *cardoncelli*, a deeply flavoured mushroom. Hoping to earn brownie points from Cleto (he had looked perplexed when I wouldn't swallow a whole squid), I wolfed down the pasta appreciatively. Hot on its heels came

Divella's Spaghetti No. 9 (classic spaghetti) with *frutti di mare*. The clean taste of the Italian parsley figured again, along with strips of squid, mussels and clams.

It is said that *olio santo* (sacred oil), a chilli-flavoured oil made by steeping hot red chillies in thick, fruity extra virgin olive oil, is potent enough to cure the plague. It is certainly revered. When the waiter brought a crock of it, Cleto gave him the nod and he ladled some of the red-tinged oil over our bowls of spaghetti. It was a real head-lifter!

Just when I thought we might be able to pause awhile, a little time to realign the sinuses perhaps, a steaming bowl of *orecchiette* was pushed under my nose. Cleto wasn't about to let us slip through Bari without trying this regional dish of small rounds of pasta. Orecchiette are native to Puglia and, like most Pugliese pastas, they have tremendous texture and chew. They were served with their classic accompaniment of turnip-top greenery, which is faintly bitter, lots of garlic and anchovies, olio santo and pools of thick fruity Pugliese extra virgin olive oil. The dish has a bold, challenging flavour; the more I ate of it, the better it got.

Cleto was hugely offended when we drew a halt at that point in the proceedings. He had charged through the dishes at an unbelievable rate of knots, consuming at least three times the amount that I had, but he was just warming up. We calmed him down by opting for some vegetable dishes and a salad. However, I could see he was thinking I was a peculiar 'foreigner' type.

I ambled over to the centre of the restaurant to admire mounds of delicious foods which I couldn't try because I was so full, but with Cleto's eyes burning into the back of my neck, I put a scoop each of zucchini *fritti* (fried discs of zucchini with masses of garlic), tiny sweet and juicy roasted capsicums cut into chunks, and marinated eggplants. Along with a palate-cleansing salad, plenty of coarse bread torn from a large crusty loaf and copious slugs of the Locorotondo, we were well and truly done for.

And so, we thought, home to bed. But no way. It was off to a local bar, where Cleto, who was a dynamic character, oozing passion from every pore, had us falling off our barstools with laughter at his yarns. But dawn would come. As he sped off into the evaporating night there was one story that stayed with me. He had explained in explicit detail how he made salami and wine in his cantina, probably illegally, and the joy this 'hobby' gave him.

At the time I thought this was quite amazing: a food export manager who wasn't even going to talk about food until we mentioned it; a person with so much knowledge about food, absorbed from his mother and his grandmother and as a result of his own enquiring mind; a man with a passion for delicious food. But over the years I discovered that this kind of encounter was common. In Italy people have a great respect for food and treat it in the best possible way. Ask any person loitering in the piazza of an Italian town, or any seller of fresh food products in the marketplace, or any shopper deliberating over a selection of parmesan cheese or olives or fresh peaches and grapes, where to buy the best food, and before you know it you'll have a group of people clustering around, offering advice on where to go, how to get there, what to look for, how to prepare it, and quoting family 'heirloom' recipes. In the culinary sense, I never met a disinterested soul on any of my numerous travels through Italy. And you can be sure the next time I'm in Bari, I'm going to get a look inside Cleto's cantina!

Cleto, this menu is for you.

PASSION FOR PUGLIA

SERVES 10

Mozzarella and Lampascioni Onions on Rocket
Green Cerignolo Olives with Roasted Red Capsicum Dressing
Stewed White Beans

Panzarotti

Mussels in Tomato Broth
Olio Santo
or
Orecchiette with Turnip-top Greenery

Fish Parcels with Olives
Roasted Fennel
Radicchio Salad

Mosquito Cake

Mussels in Tomato Broth

This is a real feast and one which requires a little planning. For me, the highlight is the antipasti; a medley of flavours, pungent, sweet, sharp and mild. With good bread, six people could dine on just this.

But we're talking *big* here, and there's plenty of antipasti for ten if served with all the following dishes. Don't contemplate rushing the food through. This is a three-hour lunch . . . and it could easily stretch longer than that.

You can chop and change the menu for small groups, or omit some of the courses. For instance, the antipasti, mussels and fish course make a balanced meal, as do the antipasti and mussels followed by the orecchiette served as a main course (you'll need to increase the quantity of orecchiette to 750 g, and serve it with a little olio santo to stretch the sauce). Alternatively, omit the antipasti, serve the panzarotti with a pre-lunch drink and serve either the mussels or orecchiette followed by the fish.

Do look for the little wild onions known as LAMPASCIONI which grow in Puglia, in particular the brand Di Giorgi. The onions are charcoal roasted and preserved in olive oil and a splash of vinegar. They are sweet and smoky with a tinge of bitterness — totally addictive (as are the Di Giorgi roasted artichokes).

The CERIGNOLO OLIVES are another specialty — big, fat and meaty, with a creamy taste. If not available, use any plump green olive (preferably Italian). Remember to put a piece of aluminium foil underneath the capsicums to catch the drips when roasting them.

PANZAROTTI (sometimes spelled panzerotti) is a typical small pastry found all over the region of Puglia. They can be made of bread dough, or a dough made with egg yolks and water, or an oil-based dough. I've given a version made with butter, egg yolks and water, because I find this easier to work with and the taste superior. Usually the pastry is cut into rounds, stuffed and folded over to form halfmoon shapes, then fried till crisp in hot oil; but sometimes the dough is shaped into small squares. When the panzarotti go into the hot oil they puff up like swollen tummies, from which they take their name. Deep-frying the panzarotti makes the pastry rich and flaky, but they can be oven-baked if you prefer. I suggest making them the day before. It's an easy matter then to finish them off just prior to serving.

I think Cleto would have approved of my version of MUSSEL BROTH — *zuppa di cozze*: mussels swimming in a gutsy tomato broth spiked with chilli. In Tuscany, olio santo is served floating on thin broths or on top of soups, but in Puglia and in Basilicata, a neighbouring province, it is added at the table, and generously, to certain pasta and seafood dishes to give them a lift. How much you add is a personal choice. Don't be alarmed by how thick the purée is initially (the mussels will give out lots of juice as they cook). This is not a regular soup, and will not look like one. Eat the mussels with the fingers, using the empty mussel shells to scoop up the tomato 'broth', and chunky bread to mop up the rest of the juices.

If mussels aren't your bag, try Puglia's famed ORECCHIETTE PASTA. These are traditionally shaped on the thumb and end up resembling little ears (hence the name). If you're lucky, you'll actually see the maker's thumbprint indented on the inside of each one. They can be dressed with a variety of sauces, but the classic treatment is to cook them with turnip-top greens and dress them with garlic and chilli sizzled in rich Pugliese extra virgin olive oil, and mashed anchovies. It's hearty peasant food.

Turnip-top greens (*cime di rape*) are a little hard to come by (some turnips are grown specifically for his purpose — gardeners might like to consider this) so I have substituted fresh spinach, which will give a milder flavour. If you *are* able to find turnip-top greens, boil them in salted water for about ten minutes before adding the orecchiette. You might like to experiment with rocket; add it to the pot of orecchiette just before draining (the quick immersion in hot water is all it needs to soften it) and finish off as described in the recipe for orecchiette.

Buy quality artisan orecchiette if you can afford it — it has much better texture, and it swells generously during cooking, giving increased bulk.

The FISH PARCELS are dead easy to prepare and there's no last-minute frying or fussing, but you have to gauge the cooking time correctly (if you're nervous, do a trial run). Make sure everyone is ready for this course before you put it in the oven. It is quick cooking — about ten minutes — and once it's ready, it can't be halted or held; the fish continues to cook once it comes out of the oven. The fish must be at room temperature before it goes in the oven, or it will take longer to cook. The pouches can be assembled up to an hour in advance; if the kitchen is not too warm, they can be kept at room temperature, but in warmer weather, keep the pouches refrigerated until 15 minutes before cooking them.

The accompaniment of ROASTED FENNEL is simply gorgeous. Roasting it makes it less aniseedy and it develops a celery-like flavour with caramel overtones. A SALAD is all that is required to balance the main course — but make something with a little interest.

Finish the meal with a slice of this unusual MOSQUITO CAKE — made with olive oil and an intriguing mix of lemon, orange, nutmeg and spice. The cake doesn't seem to suffer if it is made a day ahead; return it to the clean tin, cover the top with plastic wrap and keep at room temperature.

MOZZARELLA AND LAMPASCIONI ONIONS ON ROCKET

2–3 big handfuls of rocket leaves, washed and destalked
45 ml (3 tablespoons) extra virgin olive oil
1½ tablespoons white wine vinegar
¼ teaspoon salt
200 g bocconcini mozzarella
1 small jar charcoal-roasted lampascioni or Muscari onions, drained
Stewed white beans (recipe follows)
Green cerignolo olives with roasted capsicum dressing (recipe follows)

Strew the whole leaves of rocket over a large serving platter. Whisk the olive oil, vinegar and salt together and pour over the rocket.

Drain the mozzarella balls, pat dry with kitchen paper and slice thickly. Arrange on the rocket leaves with the onions, white beans and cerignolo olives. Serve with plenty of crusty bread.

Mozzarella and
Lampascioni Onions
on Rocket; Green
Cerignolo Olives with
Roasted Red
Capsicum Dressing;
Stewed White Beans

2 large red capsicums
500 g (2 cups) bottled green cerignolo olives, drained
2 fresh bay leaves
salt
freshly ground black pepper to taste

Put the capsicums on an oven rack in an oven preheated to 200°C and roast for about 20 minutes, or until blistered and charred. Place a piece of aluminium foil on the tray below to catch the juices as they drip.

Transfer capsicums to a plate and when cool enough to handle, peel and remove the cores and seeds. Dice the capsicum flesh and transfer it to a bowl with the juices. Add the olives, bay leaves, a pinch of salt and a little black pepper. Stir well and marinate for 2–3 hours.

STEWED WHITE BEANS

180 g (1 cup) large haricot beans
45 ml (3 tablespoons) extra virgin olive oil
1 tablespoon finely chopped rosemary
2 cloves garlic, peeled
½ teaspoon salt
freshly ground black pepper to taste

Soak the beans for 24 hours in cold water to cover. Drain, then put them in a saucepan, cover with cold water and bring to the boil. Cook at a gentle boil for 10 minutes, then drain again and transfer to a heavy-based casserole. Pour over the oil and mix in the rosemary and garlic. Pour in 2 cups of water and bring to the boil over a high heat. Remove any scum, then cover with a lid. Transfer to an oven preheated to 170°C and cook 1½–2½ hours, stirring occasionally, or until the beans are very tender.

They will probably be swimming in liquid, but most of this will be absorbed as they sit. Sprinkle over salt and grind on plenty of black pepper, stir in, then cover with a lid and leave to cool before serving. To serve, spoon beans over rocket leaves with some of the soupy juices.

Panzarotti

Makes about 35

Pastry
450 g high-grade bread flour
½ teaspoon salt
225 g butter, softened
2 medium eggs
50 ml cold water

Filling
200 g bocconcini mozzarella balls in whey
75 g prosciutto, chopped
50 g (½ cup) freshly grated parmesan cheese
pinch of salt and freshly ground black pepper to taste
1 teaspoon chopped marjoram
1 egg, lightly beaten

PASTRY

Make this first. Sift the flour and salt into a large mixing bowl. Cut the butter into small pieces and add to the flour. Cut in with two knives until the pieces of butter are very small, then rub in with your fingertips, lifting the flour up in the air as you do so to aerate it. Beat the eggs with a fork and add 25 ml of the water. Stir into the pastry and blend with a large fork. Check to see whether you need extra water by scrunching up the dough with one hand: if it feels sticky or tacky, don't add any more; if dryish, or flaky, dribble on a little more water and continue working together. (I find 40–45 mls of water with 2 medium eggs gives a perfect result.) Knead the pastry until it leaves the sides of the bowl clean, then wrap in plastic wrap and refrigerate for 2 hours. Meanwhile prepare the filling.

FILLING

Drain the mozzarella balls and pat dry with kitchen paper. Dice finely and put in a bowl with the rest of the ingredients. Mix well. Take the pastry from the fridge, cut it in two and work with one piece at a time, keeping the other covered. Roll out thinly on a floured board and stamp into rounds with a floured pastry cutter (choose a cutter about 7.5 cm in diameter). Roll each round of pastry fractionally thinner to elongate it, then stack them on a tray lined with waxed paper and chill while rolling the other half of the pastry.

Lay a dozen or so pastry rounds on a clean surface and put a generous teaspoonful of the filling over one half of each round. Dampen the edges of the pastry circles with cold water then fold over to enclose the filling, forming half circles. Press the edges together to seal then make indentations with the fork around the sealed edge. Put on a tray lined with waxed paper, cover with plastic food wrap and chill for at least 30 minutes (up to 12 hours) before baking, or freeze. Cook in batches in hot oil (180°C) for about 5 minutes until golden brown. Drain and cool briefly before serving; or, brush lightly with beaten egg and bake in an oven preheated to 180°C for about 20 minutes, or until golden brown.

SERVES 10

4 kg smallish mussels
½ cup extra virgin olive oil
4 cloves garlic, crushed
2 tiny dried bird's-eye chillies, crushed
2 x 400 g cans Italian tomatoes, mashed
½ cup dry white wine
pinch of salt
3 tablespoons coarsely chopped Italian parsley
slices of toasted ciabatta bread (optional)
olio santo (optional; recipe follows)

Scrub the mussels under running water with a stiff brush, then pull off the beards. Put the mussels in a large bowl and fill with cold water. Stir them around, then lift out into a clean bowl. Repeat this process until the water is clear and grit-free. Leave the mussels to soak for 15 minutes in fresh water. If the water is still gritty, repeat the process.

Put the oil in a large wide saucepan and add the garlic and chillies. Cook a few minutes then add the tomatoes. Bring to the boil, partially cover with a lid and cook gently for 20 minutes. Add the mussels, cover the saucepan with a lid and cook a few minutes, stirring occasionally until the mussels open (cook in batches). Transfer them to a deep serving bowl (or bowls) as they are done and keep covered with aluminium foil.

When all the mussels are ready, pour the wine into the pan, salt it lightly and allow it to bubble up. Cook 3 minutes, add the parsley then pour over the mussels. Serve immediately from the bowl, ladling mussels and juices into soup bowls or pasta plates. Serve with toasted bread and olio santo on the side.

Olio Santo

½ cup extra virgin olive oil
12 tiny dried bird's-eye chillies, crushed

Put the oil and chillies in a jar, stopper tightly, then store in a cool place for at least a week before using.

Orecchiette with Turnip-top Greenery

Serves 6–8

¾ cup extra virgin olive oil (preferably use oil from Puglia)
1½ cups fresh white breadcrumbs
salt
500 g orecchiette
700 g spinach, trimmed, washed and coarsely chopped
8 cloves garlic, chopped finely
1–2 small dried bird's-eye chillies, crushed
10 anchovies, packed in oil, drained
extra olive oil or olio santo if required

Heat a little less than half of the oil in a frying pan over a moderate heat. Add the breadcrumbs and stir until golden brown. Transfer to a plate and set aside.

Bring a large saucepan of well-salted water to the boil, drop in the orecchiette pasta and cook for 5–10 minutes or until half cooked; then add the spinach and cook for about 10 minutes more, or until the pasta is cooked. Well made artisan orecchiette may take as long as 20 minutes to cook.

A few minutes before the orecchiette are ready, heat the rest of the oil in a large frypan and gently cook the garlic, chillies and anchovies, mashing the anchovies with a wooden spoon, until the garlic colours. (The pan needs to be large enough to hold all the cooked pasta. If you don't have one large enough, omit this next step; instead, tip the orecchiette into a large heated serving bowl and pour on the hot flavoured oil. Toss and serve.)

Drain the pasta and spinach and add to the frying pan. Cook for a few minutes, mixing well, turn into hot dishes, sprinkle over the browned crumbs and serve.

If cooking 750 g orecchiette, drizzle the cooked orecchiette with more extra virgin olive oil, or olio santo, before serving.

Traditionally, parmesan cheese is not served with this dish.

Fish Parcels with Olives

Serves 10

1 small onion, finely chopped
1 large clove garlic, crushed
extra virgin olive oil
grated rind of ½ lemon
4 tablespoons chopped feathery fennel leaves (snip these off the fennel plants)
2 tablespoons chopped parsley
100 g (about 20) black olives, stoned and chopped
¼ teaspoon salt
freshly ground black pepper to taste
1.8 kg small white fish fillets, rinsed and patted dry

Put the onion and garlic in a small pan with 1 teaspoon oil and 1 tablespoon water. Cover with a lid and cook gently, stirring once or twice, till softened, then remove the lid and cook till lightly browned. Cool.

Mix the lemon rind, fennel, parsley, olives, salt and pepper in a bowl. Mix in the onion and garlic and 2 tablespoons extra virgin olive oil.

Cut 10 pieces of see-through cooking film (if not available, use baking paper) about 40 cm x 40 cm. Brush the middle of the film with oil. Cut the fish fillets into even-sized pieces and lay them in the middle of the oiled sheets. Spoon over the olive and herb mixture. Tie the packets into pouches with metal ties or opened paper clips (do not use plastic-coated ones) and transfer them to two shallow oven trays. Don't try and crowd them into one dish because it will slow down cooking and make them cook unevenly. Trim the see-through film.

Bake the fish pouches about 8–10 minutes in an oven preheated to 200°C, or until the fish is nearly cooked. Transfer to individual dinner plates and serve immediately.

Orecchiette
with Turnip-top
Greenery

ROASTED FENNEL

5 medium or 10 slim fennel bulbs
extra virgin olive oil
freshly ground black pepper

Trim the fennel bulbs then cut them in half through the root. If the bulbs are very large, cut them into quarters. Rub with olive oil and black pepper, then put them in a shallow-sided ovenproof dish, or on a baking sheet. Bake for about 30 minutes in an oven preheated to 200°C, or till tender and lightly browned. Serve warmish.

RADICCHIO SALAD

SERVES 10

3 'balls' of radicchio
½ buttercrunch or cos lettuce (optional)
3 witloof
1 cup cherry tomatoes
30 ml (2 scant tablespoons) white wine vinegar
½ teaspoon salt
freshly ground black pepper to taste
¼ teaspoon French mustard
75 ml (5 tablespoons) extra virgin olive oil

Prepare the salad items. Wash and dry the radicchio leaves and lettuce leaves (if using), put them in a plastic bag and chill until required. At serving time, prepare the witloof by trimming the ends (gouge out a little of the cores if they seem woody) then breaking the witloof apart into leaves. If the leaves are very long, cut them in half or into thirds.

Put the witloof in a salad bowl with the cherry tomatoes, radicchio and lettuce leaves torn into bite-size pieces. In a small bowl whisk together the vinegar, salt, pepper and mustard then blend in the oil. Pour over the salad, toss well and serve.

MOSQUITO CAKE

2 large eggs, at room temperature
125 g castor sugar
grated rind of 1 lemon
grated rind of 1 orange
good grating fresh nutmeg
⅛ teaspoon mixed spice
¼ teaspoon fennel seeds
50 ml fruity white wine
100 ml milk
125 ml extra virgin olive oil
200 g flour
pinch of salt
1 teaspoon baking powder
icing sugar to finish

Break the eggs into a wide bowl, beat lightly, then beat in the sugar a little at a time. Continue beating until the mixture becomes thick and pale in colour and will form a ribbon (thick trail) when the beaters are lifted up; this is easiest done with an electric beater. Add the grated lemon and orange peel, the nutmeg, mixed spice, fennel seeds, white wine, milk and olive oil. Mix thoroughly.

Sift the flour, salt and baking powder together onto a sheet of paper. Sift half of the dry ingredients into the bowl. Gently mix together with a large spoon then sift over the rest of the dry ingredients and fold in. The mixture should be thick and smooth; stir, don't beat.

Turn into a lightly oiled 22–23 cm ring mould with a 1600 ml capacity. Bake 35–40 minutes in an oven preheated to 180°C. Gently loosen from the tin, cool 10 minutes then turn out carefully onto a cake rack. When cool, dust with icing sugar and serve.

SICILIAN SPLENDOUR

SOME FRIENDLY SICILIANS AND 'THE COUCH'

My first impression of Sicily was a good one, and it has lasted. I had long been drawn by the fascinating mix of the island's wild beauty and its exotic cuisine. The exaggerated myths about the dangers of the place added to the intrigue.

Early one November Remo and I took the half-hour train-on-a-boat ride from Villa San Giovanni on the mainland of Italy to the sprawling city of Messina, then took a left turn out of Messina and headed south along the coast. The beauty of Sicily unfolded before us. Bougainvillea in a hundred shades of red and mauve clung to every nook and cranny. There were fields of tall alyssum waving in the breeze, majestic palm trees, and citrus groves which filled the air with a clean sweet perfume. It was breathtaking.

In due course we arrived at Taormina, an idyllic spot, perched 200 metres above sea level. The town hangs out like a balcony over the sea, and from it you can view the beaches below. Although it is geared to the tourist market, Taormina has irresistible charm. The shops are full of jewellery made of the black lava from nearby Mt Etna, and *pupi* (puppets) styled like Saracen invaders; and the many *vicoli* (little streets) are worth exploring.

We wandered around the main square in euphoric mood and settled on eating in a closed-in restaurant, as the weather was turning bad. I didn't need any encouragement to eat eggplant — the Sicilians are masters of eggplant cookery, and I intended to try as much as I could while in Sicily — so I chose an unusual pasta dish featuring it: spaghetti in tomato sauce and cheese, rolled in fried slices of eggplant. Not to be outdone, Remo chose another pasta, tubed *penne*, with a creamy sauce of capsicums. Both were outstanding.

These dishes were preceded by antipasti. Not wanting to repeat the stunt I had pulled at the restaurant in Alberobello, and with Remo glaring at me over the top of the menu, I ordered only four items from the tempting range: fat, green olives tasting of fruit, not salt, shimmering in their own oil; slices of sautéd zucchini; creamy, nutty-tasting eggplant slices baked in the oven; and cubes of eggplant *trifolati*, fried in olive oil with parsley and garlic. I can't deny it, I'm an eggplant addict.

This meal unexpectedly turned into a feast. We broke off chunks of crusty bread to dunk into the juices of the antipasti, knocked back copious glasses of crisp Corvo wine, and followed the pasta with grilled swordfish and a salad. A good meal certainly gives you a benevolent feeling about a place.

On our way to Palermo, we decided to visit the parents of a friend, in the small town of Barcellona on the coast southwest of Messina. Barcellona back then (I doubt it has changed) seemed caught in a time warp — the people, mostly peasants, looked hard-working and stooped, with skin like parchment. Most of the women were dressed in black to show respect for dead loved ones, a custom which seems to be fading in mainland cities.

We eventually found Signor and Signora Imbesi, and in no time at all we were ensconced in their sitting room, the happy recipients of their warm Sicilian hospitality. They were in the process of renovating an apartment for their son, Sebastiano (our friend), in an effort to entice him back to their beloved Sicilia. They offered us the apartment for as long as we wanted — 'But,' they murmured apologetically, 'there is no bed.' There was, however, a couch which folded down to a double bed, so we carried our luggage and some bed linen to the apartment, then went back to their place for an evening meal.

Signor Imbesi's eyes twinkled as he offered us home-cured olives which he had gathered from uncultivated olive trees around his home and preserved in his own kitchen. They were deliciously juicy and fruity. Meanwhile, Signora Imbesi lit a small barbecue, set about 25 cm off the ground, in the airy courtyard. She crouched on the marble-tiled floor as she got the fire going, refusing help from the menfolk. After a bit of coaxing it gave off a mean heat. Onto it she flung joints of wild rabbit which had been doused in olive oil and garlic. She used a branch of wild oregano as a brush to anoint them from time to time. A generous sprinkling of salt and pepper and they were ready — wild rabbit, barbecued Sicilian-style. Anticipating our hunger, she also threw on a few pork fillets which, with the same simple treatment, tasted extraordinarily good. We sat down to eat while she continued cooking and waited on us; offering help would have been an insult.

A salad of small leafy greens and a coarse loaf of bread were also on the table, and of course, wine. Signor Imbesi had trodden the grapes himself to make this brew. At first it tasted odd, with its strong floral bouquet and thin, chalky character — certainly not something to quaff; but when I drank it with food its magic was revealed. The bouquet opened up and became more like a fresh meadow; and its spiciness coped with garlic, strong cheese and peppered salami. It met its match with a strong *pecorino*, a cheese made up in the hills in the traditional way, from sheep's milk. We somehow managed fruit, nuts and coffee, then staggered up the road to our apartment.

Spaghetti
Taormina-style

SICILIAN SPLENDOUR • 119

And there the couch greeted us. In we hopped — but what a disaster. It was too short, too narrow, had lumps and ridges everywhere and the pillows were made of coarse straw. It was the worst night's sleep we had had in a long time. Eventually we dissolved into fits of giggles and resigned ourselves to whiling away the small hours joking about life.

Next day, eyelids propped up with matchsticks, we went back to the Imbesis' for lunch, to be greeted by the tantalising aroma of tomato sauce and, you guessed it, frying eggplant. What Signora Imbesi did with these ingredients was exceptional. She made a pie with ridged tubular pasta, *millerighe*, layered with fried eggplant and a spicy, oily tomato sauce. The strong cheese aroma came not from parmesan, but from sundried aged ricotta — a long-keeping, pungent cheese.

PALERMO AND THE VUCCIRIA MARKET

We arrived in Palermo late on a bright November day. I had expected a rundown, shabby place, but instead I found a gracious city which still proudly mirrored its glorious past. The opera house is stunning, and some of the monuments, cathedrals and other buildings are so spectacular, they gave me giant goosebumps.

We made our way to the Vucciria market early one morning. The freshness and variety of produce is stunning. We saw mounds of snow-white cauliflower, broccoli in every shade of purple and green, thatches of trimmed cardoons (a ragged celery-like vegetable), buckets of cooked potatoes floating in cold water, and huge roasted onions with their skins on. These last two seemed a little unusual, but the locals were buying plenty. Enormous shiny capsicums in shades of red, green, yellow and orange caught my eye, and round and cylindrical eggplants in purple, mauve and white. Some stalls sold nothing but olives: black, green, khaki, shrivelled or plump, in oil or brine.

The stalls stretched on and on: pears, apples, tiny coconuts, pineapples, bright yellow bananas, mountains of fennel and tight-budded artichokes, branches of grapes, prickly heaps of figs of India (prickly pears), translucent persimmons threatening to burst and spill their juice; and as for the mushrooms — some were bigger than a dinner plate.

IL FAMOSO BANDITO

When Remo took the Montelepre exit off the Palermo–Trapani motorway, I thought he must have decided to show me the setting of Mario Puzzo's novel, *The Sicilian* (the story of Giuliano Salvatore, the most infamous bandit–hero–politician in Sicily's modern history). Big deal, I thought, another Godfather story; but when Remo introduced me to Giuseppe Sciortino, the nephew of 'The Sicilian' himself, and I realised Giuliano was not just a figment of Puzzo's imagination, I started to feel uneasy.

My fears were unfounded — Signor Sciortino turned out to be a very friendly chap. He offered us coffee, and showed us photos, diaries and correspondence from his famous uncle; and he assured us that we could rely on him to furnish us with information for a 'real' Sicilian movie, not like the one, he said scathingly, which was shot down the road in another village, mocked up with the Montelepre road signs.

Giuliano Salvatore's name has now been cleared of any shady goings-on (it's amazing how death can clean the slate!) and he is now honoured as Sicily's most important independence fighter. The house where he lived is being transformed by Signor Sciortino into a tourist attraction, called Giuliano's Castle, complete with restaurant, accommodation and original chattels, and is perhaps the only reason (apart from the bread shop) to stop at this small village.

For something different, take a walk through the whitewashed villages of Trapani and enjoy a meal of *couscous* in a local restaurant. The Sicilian version of this Arabic dish, *cuscus*, consists of semolina pellets steamed over a flavoursome broth. The semolina is served with the broth, along with added fish or vegetables. In Sicily it is traditionally made with fish instead of meat, and is to be found only in and around Trapani.

In the evening, go down to the wharf area at Trapani, where the ferries leave for Sardinia and Tunisia. As darkness falls, the air is filled with thick smoke as chestnut hawkers roast their chestnuts in tall narrow cylinders with a metal bucket on top, which turns ashy inside from past roastings when heated. The nuts are placed in the bucket and as they roast they turn ash white and develop a smoky flavour.

THE CUISINE OF SICILY

Pasta and bread are two staples in Sicily, and are made from locally grown wheat. The Sicilians use both in ingenious ways, to make a little go a long way. Rice is rarely used, except in arancini, in spite of the fact that it was introduced into Italy through Sicily.

Fish is plentiful. The sea near Trapani provides ample tuna fish for Sicily and also for the mainland. In the straits of Messina, between the mainland and Sicily, great quantities of swordfish are caught — the grilled steaks are deliciously creamy. Sardines, salt cod, red mullet, freshwater fish from Syracuse and crustaceans are also plentiful. Not much meat is eaten, although there is plenty of rabbit (especially good 'sweet and sour') and pork products, including pork sausages, which are flavoured with fennel seeds and are very tasty.

Olive oil is used generously, as are olives. Butter is not used for cooking: the small amount of cow's milk produced is used in cheesemaking. Restaurants all over Sicily offer grated aged ricotta cheese with pasta dishes, in place of parmesan cheese. It smells very floral and assaults the nostrils with its pungent sting, but it matches the gutsy flavours of the food, and is easy to get addicted to.

The island is famous for its prolific crops of top-quality citrus fruit, as well as almonds, pistachios, pinenuts, grapes, sultanas, figs, artichokes, capsicums, peas, eggplants and capers. Spiced up with cinnamon, cloves, mint, aniseed and fennel, the cuisine is the most exotic in all of Italy. Vegetables and fruits grow quickly in the sunny climate and are juicy and full of flavour. Picnics of nothing but bread, tomatoes and fruit can seem like a feast, the ingredients are so good.

What permeates the cuisine, more than the liberal use of garlic, olive oil, tomatoes and eggplants, is the attitude the Sicilians have to food: they are happy to share their last crust with you. If you are invited into a Sicilian home, you go as an honoured guest; but make sure you are hungry, as they will give you their best and they won't want to see it wasted.

With its spectacular scenery, clear coastal waters, exceptional produce and friendly people, Sicily is truly a paradise!

SICILIAN SPLENDOUR

SERVES 6

Bruschetta with Tomato and Orange

Spaghetti Taormina-style

Baked Fish with Salmoriglio Dressing
Potato and Pinenut Croquettes
or
Rabbit with Sweet and Sour Sauce
Potato Purée with Olive Oil and Garlic

Green Bean and Yellow Capsicum Salad

Ricotta Crostata

Ricotta Crostata

When tomatoes are at their peak, when they have had plenty of summer sun on them to sweeten their juice, try them sliced on BRUSCHETTA (toasted ciabatta bread), topped with juicy chunks of orange. I first had this in an Italian restaurant in Melbourne, Australia. It's extraordinarily good.

The idea of rolling SPAGHETTI, which is tossed with tomato sauce, in fried rounds of eggplant shows off the Sicilian's skill with these ubiquitous ingredients. The fried eggplant and cheese make the dish rich and satisfying; serve small portions. Although it's not traditional, it can be made less rich by oven-baking the eggplant slices instead of frying them (pages 84–85).

The method of cooking fish described in the SALMORIGLIO recipe is the simplest way I know, and produces fish of delicate flavour and exceptional tenderness. Rinse the fish inside and out, season inside the cavity with a little salt, then wrap it in see-though cooking film. The fish steams in its own juices and emerges melt-in-the-mouth tender. The good thing about the see-though film is that you can see how the cooking is going. For a medium-sized fish, a rule of thumb is that when the fish eye turns white, the flesh will be just cooked through. With a smaller or larger fish, this is not such a reliable test. You'll need a small pointy knife to dig into the fleshiest part of the fish, cutting down to the bone. The fish should be about 80 per cent cooked, no more, because it will continue to cook while you arrange and serve it, due to residual heat. The fish can be barbecued or oven-baked if you prefer.

SALMORIGLIO is a dressing made by whisking boiled water into extra virgin olive oil and flavourings of lemon juice, garlic and parsley. It's the quintessential Sicilian dressing for fish.

With all this tenderness around, you need a crisp contrast to give the menu interest. The POTATO CROQUETTES, studded with pinenuts and flavoured with marjoram, are easy to do and even easier to eat. Pinenuts become rancid very quickly: buy them in small quantities and store them in the freezer.

Preparing food with an AGRODOLCE SAUCE (sweet and sour sauce) is an ancient way of cooking, popular in Sicily. Rabbit is slow to brown in olive oil, so I have added a little butter, but this is not traditional, and is optional. The delicious sauce of pinenuts, sultanas, sugar and vinegar brings the dish a touch of the exotic. In Sicily, bread would be used to mop it up, but I have given a recipe for POTATO PURÉE enriched with garlic and olive oil to serve with the rabbit for a special occasion. Both these main courses can be followed with a crisp GREEN BEAN AND SWEET YELLOW CAPSICUM SALAD, served warm.

The RICOTTA CROSTATA contains chocolate, ricotta, raisins and glacé fruits, and is perfumed with Sicily's vinous pride and joy, Marsala: it will disappear very quickly. Because the raisins are in such a different context, they don't seem repetitive after the sultanas in the agrodolce sauce.

Bruschetta with Tomato and Orange

ciabatta loaf
2 fresh cloves garlic, peeled
ripe outdoor tomatoes
juicy oranges
extra virgin olive oil (choose an estate-bottled oil with a fruity taste)
salt and freshly ground black pepper to taste

To make bruschetta, slice the ciabatta and toast the slices on a barbecue or in the oven. Rub the bruschetta with a cut clove of garlic and arrange sliced tomatoes and oranges on top. Drizzle with oil, grind on some pepper and sprinkle with salt. Serve immediately.

Spaghetti Taormina-style

Serves 4–6

3 large eggplants
salt
olive oil
1½ cups homemade tomato sauce (I like to use a puttanesca sauce)
freshly ground black pepper to taste
2 tablespoons finely chopped basil or parsley
1 small clove garlic, crushed
200 g spaghetti or spaghettini
150 g fresh bocconcini mozzarella, drained and thinly sliced
¼ cup freshly grated parmesan cheese

Cut the eggplants lengthwise into 1 cm thick slices. Layer them in a colander, sprinkling each layer with salt, and leave to drain for 40 minutes. Rinse, pat dry, then brush with oil. Place slices on an oiled baking sheet in an oven preheated to 225°C and bake about 20 minutes, or until they turn a rich golden colour.

In a bowl mix together ¾ cup of the tomato sauce, the black pepper, basil and garlic. Cook the pasta in plenty of boiling salted water until just al dente. Drain it well then toss with the sauce. Cool.

Assemble the eggplant rolls by wrapping a small amount of spaghetti in each slice of eggplant. Sit the rolls seamside down in a shallow, lightly oiled baking dish and spread the remaining sauce over them. Cover with the sliced bocconcini and sprinkle the parmesan over.

The eggplant rolls can be prepared to this point 2–3 hours ahead of time; cover and keep cool, but not refrigerated, until you are ready to serve them. Cook the rolls under a hot grill until the cheese melts and turns lightly golden. Serve immediately.

BAKED FISH WITH SALMORIGLIO DRESSING

1 medium-sized whole white fish, scaled and gutted

Rinse the fish thoroughly under running water, drain then pat dry with absorbent kitchen paper. Fish can be baked, steamed or barbecued. If baking or barbecuing, brush with oil, and baste during cooking.

Preheat oven to 190°C. Wrap fish in see-through cooking film and lay it in a large ovenproof dish. Cook about 25 minutes, or until the flesh is nearly cooked through (see menu notes). Unwrap the fish immediately and drain off the liquid. When it is well drained turn it carefully onto a large platter and pour over about one third of the salmoriglio dressing. Serve immediately with the rest of the dressing.

SALMORIGLIO DRESSING

30 ml boiling water
75 ml extra virgin olive oil
1½ tablespoons lemon juice
¾ teaspoon salt
2 cloves garlic, very finely chopped
2 tablespoons finely chopped parsley

The dressing can be prepared while the fish is in the oven. Put the oil in a bowl and beat in the boiling water slowly, using a wire whisk. Whisk in the lemon juice, salt, garlic and parsley. Pour over the fish and serve immediately.

If you want to make the dressing ahead of time, rewarm it gently at serving time either in a bowl set over a saucepan, or in the microwave.

Bruschetta
with Tomato
and Orange

POTATO AND PINENUT CROQUETTES

SERVES 6–8

1 kg floury potatoes
salt
60 g butter
6 tablespoons pinenuts
3 eggs
2 tablespoon chopped fresh marjoram
4 tablespoons freshly grated parmesan cheese
freshly ground black pepper to taste
½ cup dry breadcrumbs
olive oil

Peel potatoes and cut into chunks. Cook in salted water until tender, then drain and pass through a mouli-légumes; or mash by hand. Mix in the butter then cover with a piece of absorbent paper and leave to cool for 20 minutes.

Put the pinenuts in a shallow ovenproof dish and toast in oven at 180°C for about 10 minutes or until lightly browned. When cool, chop finely.

Separate the eggs, dropping the yolks into a cup and the whites into a shallow dish. Mix the yolks into the potatoes with the marjoram, pinenuts, parmesan, ½ teaspoon salt and pepper. Leave for 30 minutes at room temperature then mix and shape into balls. Lightly beat the egg whites with a fork. Dip the potato croquettes in the egg whites, then roll them in the dry crumbs (use a different hand for each operation).

The croquettes should be cooked within a few minutes of coating them with crumbs. Heat plenty of olive oil in a large frypan over a medium heat, and when hot, put in half the potato croquettes. Cook until golden, then turn carefully and cook the other side. When they are golden, remove to a side plate lined with crumbled kitchen paper, using a slotted spoon. Cook the second batch of croquettes. Serve hottish.

POTATO PURÉE WITH OLIVE OIL & GARLIC

1200 g potatoes, peeled
salt
2 cloves garlic, crushed
75 ml (5 tablespoons) extra virgin olive oil

Cut the potatoes into smallish, even-sized cubes and put in a saucepan. Cover generously with cold water, add some salt, then boil gently until tender. Drain well and pass them through a mouli-légumes. Beat in a teaspoon of salt and the garlic then beat in the olive oil a tablespoon at a time. Serve immediately.

SERVES 4–6

MARINADE

2 cups dry red wine
1 large onion, sliced
1 clove garlic, roughly chopped
1 teaspoon black peppercorns
sprig each parsley and thyme
1 bay leaf

SWEET AND SOUR MIXTURE

2 level tablespoons castor sugar
½ cup white wine vinegar
¼ cup raisins or sultanas
¼ cup pinenuts
1 tablespoon finely chopped parsley

MAIN INGREDIENTS

1 rabbit, cut into joints
2 tablespoons olive oil
50 g butter (optional; or increase amount of oil)
4 tablespoons plain flour
1 onion, finely chopped
2 cloves garlic, crushed
150 ml water
1 teaspoon salt
freshly ground black pepper
1 bay leaf

Put all marinade ingredients in a saucepan and slowly bring to the boil. Remove from the heat and cool. Put the rabbit joints in a bowl and pour the marinade over, then leave 2–3 hours, turning occasionally; keep covered and refrigerated.

Remove the rabbit joints from the marinade and pat dry with kitchen paper. Heat the oil in a large heavy-based casserole over a medium-high heat and drop in half the butter. Coat half the rabbit joints with flour and drop into the casserole. Brown on all sides, then transfer to a plate. Repeat with remaining rabbit joints. Add the rest of the butter to the casserole then add the onion and garlic and cook until golden. Sprinkle over the remaining flour. Stir with a spoon, then strain the marinade and add to the casserole. Add the water, salt, pepper and bay leaf. Bring to the boil, stirring, then return the rabbit joints to the casserole and bring to the boil again. Cover with a lid and cook in oven preheated to 180°C for approximately 40 minutes, or until tender. Remove casserole from oven and keep covered on oven top while making sweet and sour mixture.

SWEET AND SOUR MIXTURE

Melt the sugar slowly in a small heavy-based saucepan and allow to colour to a light golden brown. Carefully pour in the vinegar. The sugar will set hard, but keep it over a gentle heat, stirring occasionally, until it has dissolved. Add the raisins or sultanas and allow to steep 2–3 minutes then mix through the pinenuts. Remove the bay leaf from the casserole then blend in the sweet and sour mixture. Sprinkle with parsley and serve immediately in the casserole.

Green Bean and Yellow Capsicum Salad

Serves 6

2 large yellow capsicums
salt and freshly ground black pepper
1 tablespoon basil plus a sprig or two for garnishing
30 ml (2 tablespoons) extra virgin olive oil
400 g green beans, topped and tailed

Roast capsicums as described on page 50. When peeled and cored, transfer to a board (reserve all the juices in the dish) and cut into chunks. Add ¼ teaspoon salt, plenty of black pepper, basil and olive oil to the capsicum juices in the dish. Mix together, then add the capsicums. Plunge the beans into a saucepan of salted boiling water. Cook uncovered until tender. Drain, refresh with water and drain again. Pat dry with kitchen paper, then add to the dish of capsicums while still warm. Toss gently.

Ricotta Crostata

Serves 6–8 (serve at room temperature)

50 g raisins
125 g (¾ cup) glacé fruits (include something tangy such as tangelo or orange peel)
60 ml (4 tablespoons) dry Marsala
400 g sweet shortcrust pastry
450 g ricotta cheese
50 g castor sugar, plus a little extra
1 small egg, plus 2 egg yolks (reserve a little egg white for the pastry glaze)
50 g dark chocolate, roughly chopped
finely grated rind 1 lemon

Put the raisins and coarsely chopped glacé fruits in a bowl and pour on the Marsala. Leave to macerate one hour. Roll out the pastry and line a 21 cm flan ring or loose-bottomed tin. Lightly prick the pastry then chill. Gently knead any scraps of pastry together and roll out thinly then cut into long strips about 0.5 cm wide. Lay flat on a tray and chill. When pastry is firm (after about 40 minutes) line the pastry case with a double thickness of crumpled tissue paper. Bake blind 15 minutes in oven preheated to 180°C. Remove from the oven, lift off the paper and beans and cool. Pass the ricotta cheese through a sieve into a large bowl then beat in the sugar. Add the whole egg and egg yolks and beat until light. Mix in the chocolate and lemon rind and lastly the macerated fruit. Turn into the pastry case and smooth the surface with a knife. Lay the strips of pastry on top in a lattice pattern, sticking them to the pastry edge with a little cold water. Lightly beat a little egg white until fluffy then brush over the pastry strips and edge. Sift over a little castor sugar then put in the oven and bake at 180°C for about 30 minutes, or until the pastry is golden brown. Cool briefly then remove from tin and cool.

TALES OF THE OLIVE TREE

THE VERSATILE OLIVE

When I grew up there was a secret corner in my mother's kitchen that I liked to fossick in. Tucked in behind an alcove was her purse, her red lipstick, a pale pink comb with huge teeth, her copy of the *New Zealand Country Women's Institutes Cookery Book* (price 5/-), her mottled blue recipe notebook full of cutout recipes and handwritten notes, some pens, stubby pencils, and bobbypins, a large backdoor key and an innocuous brown tightly-stoppered bottle of olive oil.

My mother used the oil lavishly on her hands and nails to keep them soft and supple, and if anyone complained of an earache, she warmed some of it in an old teacup, dipped a cottonwool ball in the oil and plugged the ear with it.

It wasn't until I took a part-time job in a very smelly Greek–Bulgarian delicatessen that I became aware that olive oil was primarily a culinary ingredient, not a medicinal cure-all.

East Europeans came in regularly to buy olives ladled out of barrels of murky brine, feta dripping whey as it was scooped out of enormous shiny cans, salted anchovies, bottles of olive oil with indecipherable labels and, the stinkiest thing of all, dried salt cod. On Friday evenings they would come in with their kids swinging off their limbs, and while they argued passionately with Costa, the owner, about the 'exorbitant' price he wanted for some morsel they coveted, the kids would run riot in the shop, fuelled by exotic tidbits passed to them behind Costa's back by his gracious old father. The smell of real coffee teased my nostrils for the first time in that shop. It was fascinating.

Eventually curiosity got the better of me, and soon I was sampling the merchandise (with Costa's approval, of course). It was about this time that I started reading Elizabeth David, after which there was no turning back.

Perhaps the love of the olive is more obvious in Italy than in other Mediterranean countries. Certainly the olive oil bottle is tipped very generously onto food. But in Italy it is used not just as a cooking medium and condiment or flavouring, but as an enrichment, a nourishment, a food.

GROWING, HARVESTING AND CURING OLIVES

Although a tree will eventually sprout from an olive stone, these days most olive trees are grown from cuttings. It takes several years for a tree to establish itself, but it will then go on producing olives for many years to come, and may live for hundreds, even thousands, of years. The trees are evergreen, shedding old leaves approximately every three years to make way for new growth. Blossoms appear annually in springtime but the clusters of white flowers can easily be damaged by rain, reducing the olive harvest. The olives take several months to mature, during which time they change from green to a blackish shade when fully ripe.

Some varieties of olives, such as the Spanish *manzanilla*, are best picked and eaten green, while others, such as the Greek *kalamata*, are best fully ripe. Some contain more oil than others and are pressed to produce olive oil. Fleshier varieties are more suited to curing and eating as table olives.

The method for harvesting olives has remained unchanged for centuries. Traditionally the fruit is plucked by hand and dropped into a net below. This ensures that each olive is harvested at its optimum ripeness and that the fruit is not damaged. However, when the olives are going to be pressed to extract oil they are usually knocked from the trees with sticks (it's faster than hand-picking but still labour-intensive). Mechanical harvesters, although much faster than these two methods, are not selective. They shake the whole crop from the tree, in varying stages of ripeness, leaving behind only the stubborn fruit, which need to be knocked off with a stick anyway. The olives are then sorted to separate out any leaves or twigs. They are weighed then washed as soon after picking as possible, to ensure fermentation doesn't begin.

Fully ripe black olives can be preserved immediately in brine, or cured in dry salt, but green olives need soaking in a soda solution first, with plenty of washing and rinsing to leach out the bitter glucosides before preserving in brine. Both types are ready for eating after about a month; or they can be preserved in oils flavoured with herbs, garlic or spices.

If you have a batch of olives which are too salty, soak them in water for about a week, changing the water daily. They can be further improved by marinating them in olive oil with seasonings.

It's worth noting that olive oil is the only vegetable oil which is edible immediately after pressing. Other seed oils have to be treated to remove toxins before they are fit to eat.

PRESSING FOR OIL

First, cold-pressed olive oil is obtained from sound olives, which are washed then put through the olive mill. In times gone by the resulting paste was spread on mats, which were then placed in a hydraulic press. The pressed mixture was separated by centrifugation into oil and water, and the oil was poured off. These days, the olives go in one end of a machine and emerge at the other as oil. At this point the oil is usually filtered (unfiltered oils

Pinzimonio

are sometimes sold in the market place). The oil is known as virgin olive oil and it is graded according to the acidity level.

The solid matter which is left from the first cold pressing of olives is used to make refined oil. It is heated with water and pressed again, sometimes twice, producing an olive oil with less flavour and aroma and with a higher acidity. The oil is then further refined, either with chemicals or by centrifuge. The oil may then be bleached or filtered. This 'pure' olive oil is then mixed with virgin olive oil to improve its quality.

TUSCAN MEMORIES

There is an old Tuscan adage: 'Where there is good oil, there is good wine.' I discovered this in reverse — that is, I found the good wine first. I'm going to tell you about a special meal I had at the Selvapiana Estate in Rufina, Tuscany, a charming village northeast of Florence at the home of Dr Francesco Giuntini. When I made an appointment to interview Dr Giuntini, an agronomist, about his wine, he asked me and Remo to come for lunch. The Selvapiana Estate produces excellent Chianti, and falls within one of the seven denominations allowed for in the Chianti DOC (*Denominazione di Origine Controllata*, which certifies that wines with this label are made from grapes grown in a defined production zone and comply with specific quality measures).

'Dr Giuntini' soon gave way to Francesco and 'Signora Biuso' to Julie. I was introduced to 'Cook', who was producing some tantalising smells in the kitchen; then it was down to the cellars with Francesco, who was dressed for the autumn chill in long grey coat and snug hat. The cellar smelled of earth and squished grapes, and a pungent smell of alcohol filled the air. The cellar was being used to house wines from the vintages of 1971–86, but there were a few racks of old bottles, *c.* 1928, covered in so much dust that at first glance the labels were unreadable. Francesco insisted we take a bottle of Selvapiana Chianti Reserva from the excellent 1968 vintage home with us to New Zealand. It would have been impolite to refuse.

While we were waiting for lunch we took a stroll through the grounds. The sight of swollen blackened tree stumps was distressing. He explained that many of the Estate's mature fruit-bearing olive trees were destroyed during the crippling frosts of 1985. He spoke of his olive oil with reverence, then, sensing that I was serious about it, took me back down to another cellar to show me the olive presses and *esparto* mats on which the olive paste is spread out to dry. The air was redolent with olive fruit, although very little had been pressed this season. The smell seemed to emanate from the ancient stone walls of the cellar. Unfortunately a whiff in the wind was all I got of the Selvapiana Estate oils — there was not a drop in the cellar or kitchens to be had! Francesco was saddened that he couldn't give me any oil to take home with the wine. So was I.

Ah, well. Back up the stairs into the warmth we traipsed, to Cook and her offerings. Hunting season was in full swing and she produced two exceptional seasonal dishes: a Tuscan classic of flat pasta noodles dressed with a wild hare sauce; and a simple dish of rabbit joints, browned in olive oil and splashed with white wine, then cooked till tender. A roast of beef was also served. The beef had a small tunnel through the centre, Cook told me, made with the long rounded handle of a wooden cooking spoon, and was stuffed with rosemary and garlic, then roasted and glazed with a little Selvapiana non Reserva Chianti. There was a rich dish of creamed spinach (the spinach had been pulled from the estate garden that morning), and impossible-to-stop-eating tiny roasted potatoes.

Cheeses followed, with an apology: Francesco said he couldn't stop Cook buying French brie! This was served with firm sheep's milk cheese, which had a pleasing fresh acidity. And Cook was still just warming up: a wonderful fresh raspberry tart with a crisp pastry made a tangy-sweet finale, along with huge creamy walnuts, autumn fruits, inky black shots of coffee and a nip or two of *vin santo*, a raisiny wine made by drying the ripe grapes in the air before pressing them. We even managed to squeeze in a couple of almond biscotti to dunk in the wine.

Cook by this time had been asked to join us with her young family, who all live at the Estate. In the contented afterglow that follows an exceptional repast, she and I sat at the table swapping culinary tales and recipes.

We kept in touch, Francesco and I, over the years. It was a lovely surprise to receive a large bottle of cold pressed Selvapiana extra virgin olive oil in New Zealand, delivered by express mail (costing an arm and a leg in postage), in December 1995. He hadn't forgotten me — it had taken that long (nearly ten years) for his olive trees to recover. The oil was unlike any I have had before. Rich, thick, green and very peppery, it danced on the tongue! I was torn between wanting to keep it forever, and wanting to devour it immediately. With restricted use it lasted a month, and every time I took the bottle out and poured some of the oil on food, it transported me back to Tuscany, to the Selvapiana Estate and to the warm, friendly, down-to-earth hospitality of the Tuscans we met there.

YOU'RE NEVER TOO OLD TO LEARN

Here's another Tuscan tale which illustrates just how revered cold pressed extra virgin olive oil is around these parts. Remo and I were staying at his family's summer home, Querciolo, in Tuscany, with our son Luca around the time of his first birthday.

My brother-in-law's sister-in-law, Irene, would harvest her olives every autumn and have them crushed. The oil would be used judiciously through the ensuing months to dress vegetables, salads and fish. The batch that late summer of 1988 was thick and murky (the oil was unfiltered), a dull emerald green, smelling of ripe olives and mown grass. It was addictive.

Luca had a healthy appetite. He loved vegetables, adored pasta and became ecstatic when the two were in the same bowl together, as in minestrone. His diet up to that point had been largely fat-free. I was going to bring this child up to be healthy and strong, on unadulterated food. I'll never forget Irene's insistence that first day she came to Querciolo that I should enrich Luca's soups and vegetables with a tablespoonful of her precious oil. I wanted to protest; no fat for my boy! But looking deep into the eyes of the women gathered around, I knew I had a weak case. 'Just a spoonful,' they chanted, 'it's extremely beneficial for the baby.' They knew this instinctively. Nowadays we can quote data from research into the benefits of olive oil, but they just knew, as their forebears knew, that extra virgin olive oil is a life-giving food.

When I reflected on my response — I would have been far less concerned had my son been offered an icecream, which has more fat, as well as sugar and possibly chemicals — I realised how wrong I was. Like most mothers with their first child, I was being overprotective. I started to take notice of the old women. My second child had extra virgin olive oil and parmigiano reggiano introduced to her diet as soon as possible.

TALES OF THE OLIVE TREE

SERVES 6

Pinzimonio

Margot's Spaghetti with Olive Sauce
or
Rigatoni with Eggplant, Red Capsicum, Capers and Olives

Mamma Rosa's Polpettine
Tomato and Oregano Salad

Baked Croissant with Sugared Fruit

Mamma Rosa's Polpettine

This menu features olives and olive oil in various forms; but there are many other recipes in this book highlighting the Italians' passion for the fruit of the olive tree. PINZIMONIO is the simplest start to a meal that I know of — a platter of superbly fresh vegetables served with a bowl of seasoned olive oil. There are few rules: the vegetables must be in their prime, fresh and crisp, and the oil must be extra virgin and the best you can afford. Apart from that, you can experiment: serve just one vegetable, or a variety. With robust vegetables such as celery, fennel and carrot, try a heavier oil from Puglia; a fruity Tuscan oil with sweet red capsicums; a light, nutty oil from Liguria with raw baby artichokes, sliced thinly. In Tuscany, pinzimonio usually precedes pasta or meat, but it is served at other times in other regions, and sometimes as a nibble.

I've given a choice of two pasta dishes. The SPAGHETTI is one of those dead easy jobs that can be whipped up with no kerfuffle; it's pretty standard Italian fare. But what makes it exceptional is the tiny black Ligurian olives, which have a tinge of bitterness along with a very fruity flavour. If you can't get them, use small black olives from elsewhere in Italy or small black Niçoise olives instead.

You will need an olive pitter (available from good kitchen stores) to remove the pits. Larger olives will speed up the preparation of the sauce, but don't be tempted by pre-sliced black olives. They are usually treated with steam to remove the pits and lack flavour.

The RIGATONI dressed with a chunky eggplant sauce, studded with capers and given a sweet lift from roasted capsicum is a bit more work but well worth it. I find mounds of eggplants and capsicums irresistible when they are cheap and plentiful in late summer, and invariably buy too many; this sauce gets me out of many a culinary quandary. I also like it because you don't have to worry about frying the eggplants — they just get stirred in and sloshed around (you want the sauce to end up like a lumpy textured purée).

Both pasta dishes can be served at other times as a main course for four people, or in eight smaller portions as part of a full menu. If you want to vary the pasta type, try penne with the olive sauce. The eggplant sauce will work well on other chunky macaroni types of pasta, but it is too lumpy for spaghetti or noodles — it simply falls off, leaving a lot of sauce in the bowl. You need pasta with holes or cavities to trap the sauce.

It's an expensive business to put on the oven to roast one capsicum. I suggest you do half a dozen at the same time. Stored refrigerated, the capsicums will keep for several days and provide endless possibilities for sauces, salads and crostini.

Now something about MAMMA ROSA'S POLPETTINE. Don't think of them simply as 'meatballs'. Well flavoured with garlic and marjoram, threaded onto skewers, interspersed with crusts of toasted bread and melting globs of cheese, they're rich and delicious and need little accompaniment. Follow them with something to cleanse the palate, such as TOMATO AND OREGANO SALAD. If you must have a starchy vegetable to complete the meal, choose something which is easy to execute, such as ROASTED POTATOES WITH SEA SALT on page 63. Egging and crumbing the polpettine is easy if things are well organised to begin with. Have the crumbs and flour on separate sheets of waxed paper and the eggs in a large shallow dish. Use a spoon to help dust the polpettine with flour and a brush to coat them with egg. The quantity of coating ingredients is deliberately generous to make it easier to do the job. Some will inevitably be wasted, but it really slows you down if you work with the exact amount of beaten egg, flour and crumbs; some of the mixture gets tacky and the coating will be less than perfect. Treat the skewers carefully when moving them around the workbench, as the meatballs are delicate. There is less chance of the cheese bursting out of its crispy jacket if it is cooked while it is still well chilled. The meatball mixture can also be used as a stuffing, or shaped into small balls and roasted in a shallow oven dish in a moderate oven until browned (about 15 minutes) and served with roasted meats — children love them. The only pain with the polpettine is that they require last-minute frying. It's par for the course in Italian kitchens, but it seems to irk most non-Italian cooks. Try setting up an outside cooking area — temporary or permanent, sheltered or not depending on the weather. This gives you freedom to cook in splattering oil in a frypan over a portable gas burner. Once frying is finished, simply turn off the gas and turn your back on the splatters, as they are absorbed by the grass or trees.

Something as simple as a TOMATO SALAD doesn't need a recipe of exact measurements. What it does need is superb ripe outdoor tomatoes bursting with sweet juice; or better still, an armful of those wonderful fat green-tinged tomatoes found throughout all of Italy in late summer. Their sweet flavour, perfectly balanced with a slight acidity, should not be upset by the inclusion of vinegar or lemon. This is the place to use an exquisite estate-bottled fruity extra virgin olive oil and aromatic wild oregano from the hills of Sicily (if not available, use basil).

BAKED CROISSANTS WITH SUGARED FRUIT is a wonderful dessert — quick and easy to put together, it looks appealing and tastes divine.

GRADES OF OLIVE OIL

Virgin olive oil is broken down into grades according to the amount of acidity.
Extra virgin olive oil: virgin olive oil of sound quality (aroma and taste) with less than 1 percent acidity. It has the full flavour, colour and nutritive value of the fruit.
Fine virgin olive oil: As for extra virgin olive oil but with a higher acidity, up to 1.5 percent.
Virgin olive oil: reasonable aroma and taste, acidity up to 3 percent.
Refined olive oil: virgin olive oil which has been refined.
'Pure' olive oil: a mixture of refined olive oil and virgin olive oil.

TERMS USED TO DESCRIBE OLIVE OIL

Almondy: the oil can smell of plump, juicy almonds, but this characteristic is usually associated with taste. A little nuttiness can provide a pleasant backdrop for fruity olive flavours.
Bitter: a bitter taste can occur from green olives, or olives picked on the point of ripening. If it lingers longer than a few minutes after swallowing, it becomes unpleasant.
Buttery: a hint of butteriness can give smoothness; too much dominates other flavours.
Earthy: olives processed with earth or mud — unpleasant in any degree.
Fruity: oil which smells and/or tastes of fresh-picked, sound olives.
Grassy or hay: smelling or tasting of fresh-cut grass or stacked hay; a little can provide intrigue, too much can overpower.
Greasy: usually found in thick, heavy oils; the oil tends to coat the lips, teeth and palate.
Green leaves: from very green (underripe) olives, sometimes crushed with leaves and stalks.
Musty, mouldy, fermenting: unpleasant smells due to poor handling before processing.
Peppery: should not be confused with acidity, which is felt at the back of the throat, like a sore throat. Pepperiness is felt on the palate and can give an oil vigour, or a lift.
Rancid: an off-flavour caused by prolonged contact with air.

PINZIMONIO

extra virgin olive oil (the best quality you can afford)
salt and freshly ground black pepper to taste
fennel bulb
young carrots
red or yellow capsicums
cucumber
small radishes
celery
young artichokes
witloof

Mix together the olive oil, salt and black pepper in a small serving bowl.

Choose a selection of vegetables and prepare as described.
Fennel bulb: trim top and bottom, discard any bruised parts then cut the flesh into thick pieces.
Carrots: leave a little of the greenery on if it is fresh. Peel and cut into long fingers.
Red or yellow capsicums: Cut in half, discard core and seeds, rinse and slice into fat chunks.
Cucumber: peel if the skin is tough, halve, remove seeds then slice into long chunks.
Radishes: leave a little bit of the greenery on if it is fresh. Wash well.
Celery: use the tender middle stalks of the celery. Wash well.
Artichokes: these must be very young and tender. Slice off the stem and the top third of the artichokes, then peel away the leaves until you nearly reach the centre; the leaves should be very tender and the choke unformed. Slice into fat fingers, dropping the pieces into a bowl of water with a little lemon juice. If the artichokes have formed chokes, remove them completely, scraping them out with a sharp pointed teaspoon, and pull out any small spiky leaves in the centre. Shake well and pat dry before serving. (Leave in the water until required.)
Witloof: trim, discard outer leaves, then separate into leaves.

MARGOT'S SPAGHETTI WITH OLIVE SAUCE

SERVES 6 (as a starter or 4 as a main course)

75 ml (5 tablespoons) olive oil
3 large cloves garlic, peeled and crushed
4 tiny dried bird's-eye chillies, crushed
600 g canned Italian tomatoes, well mashed
salt
½ cup small black Ligurian olives (or small Italian olives), drained
500 g spaghetti
freshly grated parmesan cheese for serving

Put the oil in a heavy-based saucepan and add the garlic and chillies. Cook over a moderate heat till the garlic turns a pale gold colour, then carefully pour in the tomatoes. Add ¼ teaspoon of salt and bring the sauce to a gentle boil. Lower the heat and simmer for 30 minutes, or till the oil is separating from the tomatoes, and the tomatoes are thick and pulpy.

Meanwhile, remove the pits from the olives (an olive pitter or cherry stoner makes quick work of this) and chop roughly if large. Add the olives, then cook the sauce a minute or two to amalgamate the flavours. Cook the spaghetti in plenty of well salted, boiling water until al dente. Drain, tip into a heated serving dish and pour on the hot sauce. Toss and serve immediately with parmesan cheese.

If required, the sauce can be prepared a day in advance: cool, cover and refrigerate, then heat through gently when required.

RIGATONI WITH EGGPLANT, RED CAPSICUM, CAPERS AND OLIVES

SERVES 6 (as a starter or 4 as a main course)

1 red capsicum
1 small eggplant, approx 150–200 g
90 ml (6 tablespoons) olive oil
2 large cloves garlic, crushed
400 g can Italian tomatoes, mashed
1 tablespoon Italian tomato paste
¼ teaspoon of salt and freshly ground black pepper to taste
100 g (½ cup) black olives, pitted and halved
2 tablespoons capers, drained
1 teaspoon chopped marjoram (or ½ teaspoon dried marjoram)
500 g rigatoni
freshly grated parmesan cheese for serving

Roast capsicum as described on page 50. After cutting into chunks, set aside with any juices. Cut the eggplant into small cubes. Put 75 ml (5 tablespoons) of the olive oil and garlic in a heavy-based saucepan and set over a low to medium heat. Cook gently, until the garlic is a pale biscuit colour. Add the eggplant cubes and cook stirring for 2–3 minutes, then add the tomatoes, tomato paste and ¼ cup water. Add the salt and plenty of black pepper then bring to a gentle boil. Lower the heat, cover with a lid (leave a gap for steam to escape) and cook gently, stirring often, for 30–40 minutes or until the eggplant is tender. Mash the eggplant cubes a little to incorporate them into the sauce, then add the olives, capers, red capsicum and marjoram and cook 5 minutes more. The sauce can be prepared a day in advance if required; cover and refrigerate when cool.

Meanwhile, cook the rigatoni in plenty of gently boiling, well salted water until al dente. Drain briefly and turn onto a heated serving dish. Toss through the last tablespoon of extra virgin olive oil, pour on the sauce, toss well and serve immediately with parmesan cheese.

Mamma Rosa's Polpettine

Serves 6 (makes 12 skewers)

2 small red onions
approx. half a French loaf
250 g Gruyère cheese, cut into 24 cubes
600 g minced veal (or pork and veal)
50 g (½ cup) freshly grated parmesan cheese
50 g (½ cup) fresh white breadcrumbs
2 small eggs, lightly beaten
2 large cloves garlic, crushed
½ teaspoon salt
freshly ground black pepper to taste
1 tablespoon finely chopped marjoram (or ½ tablespoon dried marjoram)
12 fresh bay leaves
olive oil for frying

COATING
½ cup plain flour
3 large eggs, lightly beaten with quarter of a teaspoon of salt
1 cup dried white breadcrumbs

Cut the peeled onions in half through the root, then cut each half onion through the root lengthwise again into three pieces. Slice the French bread into thick rounds and then into 24 chunks about the same size as the cheese cubes. Set aside with the onion.

Put the minced veal in a bowl and add the parmesan cheese, breadcrumbs, beaten eggs, garlic, salt, pepper and marjoram. Mix thoroughly. Shape into 24 oval meatballs, keeping hands moist with a little water to prevent sticking.

Skewer the ingredients onto 12 skewers in this order: meatball, cube of cheese, cube of French bread, piece of onion, bay leaf folded in two, then meatball, cube of cheese and cube of French bread. Choose skewers with a maximum length of 23 cm or they won't fit in a regular frypan.

When all the polpettine are assembled, dust generously with flour then brush carefully with beaten egg and coat with dried breadcrumbs. Transfer to a flat plate.

The polpettine may be prepared several hours ahead up to this point (it's definitely advisable to do this): cover and keep refrigerated. Note that there is less chance of the cheese melting and burning if it is well chilled.

When ready to cook, heat a 1 cm depth of olive oil in a large frypan over a medium-high heat and cook 3–4 polpettine at a time (you may need to add more oil between batches). When they are golden and cooked, transfer them to a rack set over a baking dish and keep warm in a low oven; don't cover them or they will lose their crispness. (You may need to skim the oil with a small metal strainer in between cooking the batches of polpettine to remove any pieces of cheese which ooze out.) Transfer to a heated serving plate and serve hot.

TOMATO AND OREGANO SALAD

6 large ripe outdoor tomatoes
salt and freshly ground black pepper
fruity extra virgin olive oil
dried oregano from Sicily or Greece (or substitute basil)

Slice the tomatoes thickly and put in a shallow serving dish.

Just before serving, sprinkle with a little salt, grind on some pepper, drizzle with the oil then sprinkle with oregano. Serve immediately.

BAKED CROISSANTS WITH SUGARED FRUIT

SERVES 6

3 large or 6 small croissants, halved
assortment of summer fruits, 8–10 (peaches, plums, nectarines, apricots, cherries)
and some berries (raspberries, blackberries)
juice of half a lemon
castor sugar
icing sugar

Put the croissants, cut side up, in a non-stick, shallow-sided tray (a Swiss roll tin is ideal); if the tray is not non-stick, line with see-through cooking film ahead of time.

Peel, stone and slice fruit as appropriate. Put all the fruit, except the berries, in a bowl and pour over the lemon juice. Stir through one tablespoon of castor sugar, then cover and refrigerate for 2–3 hours.

Add the berries to the fruit, then spoon fruit and juices over the croissants. Sprinkle fruit generously with castor sugar. Bake immediately in an oven preheated to 200°C for about 20 minutes, or until the croissants are very crisp and the fruit softened and slightly browned.

Sift over icing sugar and serve hot or warm with cream.

MISTY MORNINGS AND MELLOW AFTERNOONS

This chapter is about damp earth, chill air, rotting leaves and blankets of mist; early morning rising; fiercely guarded patches; gumboots, flasks of adrenalin-pumping coffee, and wicker baskets lined with fresh leaves to carry the prized booty — mushrooms! *Porcini!*

Gnarled old women, scorched by the sun and stooped from working the land, impale plastic supermarket bags coloured baby blue, hot pink and burnt orange on long sticks pushed into the ground. The bags, out of tune with the breathtaking beauty of the countryside, flutter in the breeze and catch the attention of passing motorists.

You'll never see the old woman until you have stopped your car, got out and been secretly appraised. She doesn't want to be robbed of porcini, or her lire. Providing you don't inspire too great a fear in her, she'll appear from nowhere with her wicker basket, ready to flee at the slightest uncertainty.

I remember one old witch of a woman who shut the flap on her wicker basket, like a Venus flytrap, just as I was about to finger one of her porcini 'jewels'. Our eyes locked. 'Don't you dare,' she intimated. I bought the lot in case she put a hex on me for contaminating them. Paid-up and porcini-less, she fled into the roadside scrub, leaving no trace other than the flapping plastic bags.

This autumn menu celebrates the true forager — those who manage to rise from their warm bed when the alarm goes off at 4.00 am and creep around the countryside in waterlogged squelching gumboots, avoiding witches and warts and poisoned potions, hunting mushrooms.

Be warned, though, that once a *funghi* fetish takes hold, it soon mutates. A desire to try the white Alba truffle will worm its way into your subconscious, and before you can say Alitalia, you'll be winging your way to Piedmont.

SNIFFING OUT TRUFFLES

You have to have a good nose to sniff out truffles. Dogs and pigs can really get into it because they don't mind getting their noses dirty.

I once met a man with a magnificent nose. It looked like an A-grade truffle. Ashen in colour, rough and bumpy and pitted, a well matured specimen. It confirmed my suspicion that people grow to look like their pets — or their passions. Yes, this refined Piedmontese gentleman was none other than the Gran Maestro del Tartufo, the Truffle Master — an honour not lightly bestowed in Piedmont.

I met him in the gorgeous town of Alba, where truffles are taken so seriously they spend the whole month of October celebrating them. Honour is at stake. Meetings take place in the dead of night. Money changes hands in the early hours of misty mornings. Cloak and dagger (well, spade, at least), the truffle trade. In fact, the clandestine manner in which truffles are sourced and sold adds to their desirability. Then there are the rogues who will rip you off at the marketplace by poking a neat little tunnel through the truffle and filling it with dirt, which adds a few grams, and therefore extra lire, to the price.

At its best, the Piedmont white truffle is to die for — but unlike mushrooms, which some people do die for, truffles are fairly risk-free.

It's hard to put your finger on exactly what truffles smell and taste like — there's no one word for all the tantalising, complex, savoury smells, and the off-odours, which waft around it. But here's a try.

At close range the truffle smells like wood mushrooms steeped in Madeira, with hints of Vegemite and yeast — stock cubes, beefy, savoury. Rich, earthy, complex. Like a reduced sauce of garlic, shallot and mushrooms sautéd in butter, splashed with cognac and bubbled with cream. Sweet and musky. Like Maltexo, wheat germ, scalded cream. Scorched gravy, caramelised parsnips. Yes, caramel.

It's almost too much. Too heady.

Hot feet locked in sandshoes. The scrapings from the bottom of a garbage can; fetid, rank. Wet dogs on heat. Dog droppings decomposing under damp leaves. Suffocating. Cloying.

Truffles smell of all of these things some of the time; and some of these things all of the time. They are elusive little devils.

Dolce Amor

THE TRUFFLE EXPERIENCE

My first encounter with the white Alba truffle was at La Belvedere, a restaurant nestled in the hills of the lovely village of La Morra, close to Alba. It was truffle season and truffles were being sniffed out and dug up all around us. During the month of October the entire area reeks of them, a pungent and intoxicating smell.

Throughout the year the food in the Albarese restaurants is rich and homely, bursting with flavour and made with top quality produce. But it's during the month of October that the town comes alive as the locals and visitors revel in this gastronomic orgy. The Gran Maestro del Tartufo, Signor Luciano de Giacomi himself, had given us the 'nod nod, wink, wink' to go to La Belvedere for lunch, so

it was on his advice that we found ourselves ensconced in a large crowded restaurant one fine autumnal day, with one purpose in mind — to eat truffles.

Our welcoming waitress asked us if we would like to start with the antipasti. In unison we chirped 'Si', not even enquiring what it included, but one look around the restaurant at the animated locals supping and making merry assured us we were in for a treat.

A dark aromatic pâté and a terrine of wild hare and pheasant were delivered first. The pâté was oily and rich with mysterious flavours we couldn't determine. The terrine, studded with juniper berries, had a sharpish tang which cut through the richness. We wolfed them down with crusty bread. It was a good start.

A plate of *carne crude* was delivered by a waitress who, sensing out trepidation, smiled ever wider. 'It'll be alright,' her smile conveyed. Similar in appearance to steak tartare, the pale pink meat had been shredded with a fork and mixed with condiments and was, fortunately, minus the egg yolk which wobbles menacingly on top of steak tartare. It was light and tasty. I flashed the waitress a smile across the room. Good, we were doing fine.

A huge hunk of yellow capsicum, roasted in the wood-fired oven till caramelised and glistening, plus a superb salad of fresh fat porcini mushrooms, thickly sliced and dressed with lots of lemon, parsley and oil, sent us into raptures.

A thin wedge of onion frittata was next, followed quickly by a succession of hot dishes. A small sausage-shaped spinach mixture, like a spinach cream, covered with a blanket of just-melted *fontina* cheese, accompanied by a slice of *cotechino* sausage (a spicy sausage) was sensational.

It was button-popping stuff alright, but we couldn't resist the next dish of silken polenta with a spicy tomato and mushroom sauce, spiked with rosemary.

And then it happened. The truffle experience I had dreamed about. Steaming plates of fresh pasta noodles slicked with butter and parmesan cheese were put down in front of us. Where are the truffles? our eyes demanded as we looked from our plates to each other. 'Relax,' smiled the waitress, as she raised a large knobbly beige thing above my plate.

Using a special grater, she shaved off sliver after sliver of the precious stuff over the pasta, then she left us to it. Unlike black truffles, white Alba truffles are never cooked. They are brushed free of dirt then shaved directly on top of food. The slices of truffle, like soft curls of fabric, caressed the noodles as the heat of the pasta melted them. It was sensuous and intoxicating and I succumbed willingly to the pleasures of the plate.

What a splendid meal! But we could go no further. We refused a second main course of meat and vegetable dishes, and just sat and let the pleasure of the whole day wash over us and seep into our bones. After a brisk trot around the mist-shrouded hills surrounding La Morra, we were able to pour ourselves into the car and meander back to Alba.

The next day, unbelievably, we gorged ourselves again, this time at the hands of Signora Dente and her chef-husband, at the restaurant in the old castle in Castiglione, near Asti. This time the truffle made its appearance over a plate of veal *carpaccio* made with very young pale veal, sliced wafer-thin, drizzled with fruity extra virgin olive oil and seasonings. Lemon was served on the side to squeeze over the meat and it was garnished with Italian parsley and fresh bay leaves.

I was just about to tuck into the meat, when the Signora strode up to the table with the now familiar knobbly chunk of truffle. She shaved heaps of the stuff over the veal. I watched the wafer-thin slivers sit up proudly then sink into the golden green pond of oil.

I was in heaven. The aroma was powerful, and the taste was too. The truffles leave their calling card on anything they come in contact with, yet somehow, in this dish, their flavour did not overpower the veal. It was a question of balance, just enough salt, just enough lemon, the right texture and lightness to the dish.

Fresh truffles are hard to come by out of Italy, but this autumnal menu makes use of porcini mushrooms and field mushrooms. If porcini are not available, serve Zia Flavia's Pasta with Broccoli instead.

ZIA FLAVIA'S PASTA WITH BROCCOLI

The first time I met Zia Flavia in Palermo, I felt ill. Remo and I had been roaming around Italy eating anything put in front of us and we were stuffed to the gills with glorious food. When I reached Palermo my indulgences had caught up with me and I felt ready to burst.

We were to use Zia Flavia's home as a base while we travelled around Sicily, but our first meal with her was a disaster and tested her hospitality. I had seen her slaving over the stove before I went for a much-needed rest. I dreamed of waking ravenous, but it was not to be. Instead, when the cooking odours reached my nostrils and registered with my brain, I felt ill again.

The evening meal consisted of *spiedini*, a typical Sicilian dish of skewered cubes of veal, button onions and fresh bay leaves, little cubes of roasted potatoes strewn with scraps of garlic, and chunks of sautéd sweet yellow capsicums. All of this would be quite tasty under normal circumstances, but that evening the amount I ate was embarrassingly small. Explaining to Zia Flavia that it wasn't her cooking, simply that we were literally stuffed, did not appease her.

The worst insult you can given any Italian who invites you into their home is to refuse their food. They will remain convinced that it is not good enough until you relent and try some, and hopefully go for seconds. If you eat everything they make you, they'll be buoyant.

Once Zia Flavia had swept the tablecloth free of breadcrumbs, she rolled out what she thought would be the *pièce de résistance*, an elaborate Sicilian *cassata*. Looking at it made my cavities twinge.

Sicilian cassata is not made with icecream. It is made with sugar. The bulk is an incredibly sweet sponge soaked in vermouth or sweet liqueur, layered with sweetened ricotta and nuggets of chocolate. This is wrapped in almond paste then drizzled with glacé icing. The lot is then decorated with candied fruits and fine strips of 'angel hair', made by candying pumpkin until it turns white. I *had* to have a slice of it. It was the sweetest dessert I've ever eaten and I went to bed dreaming of water — water in my mouth, water splashing my face, water to wash the sweetness away.

I was forgiven for being so despondent towards Zia Flavia's cooking only when the cause was revealed: '*Un bambino? O gioa mia!* (A baby? Oh, my darling!)'. Get pregnant in Italy and you'll be forgiven almost anything. I owe it to her to include at least one of her original and well executed dishes in this book.

MISTY MORNINGS AND MELLOW AFTERNOONS

SERVES 6

Rigatoni with Isanna's Porcini Ragù
or
Zia Flavia's Pasta with Broccoli

Pheasant with Field Mushrooms
Fried Jerusalem Artichoke Chips
Smothered Cabbage
or
Guinea Fowl with Raisins and Red Wine
Grilled Radicchio
Mamma Rosa's Spinach
Stewed Lentils

Dolce Amor

From top left: Smothered Cabbage; Fried Jerusalem Artichoke Chips; Pheasant with Field Mushrooms

've mentioned elsewhere in this book about Isanna's skill in the kitchen — fresh pasta and pasta sauces are her specialty. Porcini are very dense mushrooms, with a strong woodsy aroma and taste. Eaten fresh, they are not soft and tender like field mushrooms, but have a meaty texture. You can make a meal of one large porcini mushroom, crumbed and fried till golden and served with nought else but a squirt of lemon (the vegetarian steak). These aromatic funghi are used raw in salads, and can be stuffed, baked or grilled, served on top of pasta or polenta as well as in risottos and in sauces to go with game and meat. Dried porcini are reconstituted in warm water to soften them and used in sauces and risottos. Drying the funghi seems to concentrate the savoury aromas and tastes.

At the height of the funghi season, in late autumn, Isanna starts keeping an eye on the porcini in the market. When they are at their peak, and at their lowest price, she buys a huge basket of them to dry for winter use. After checking them for grit, she lays them out on a large scrubbed wooden plank and moves them around the house from one warm spot to another over a period of about two weeks. She then threads them together and hangs them in the wine cellar and uses them to brighten meals during the chilly months. They are reconstituted in warm water, which softens them, then incorporated, usually along with the filtered soaking liquid, into cooked dishes. The PORCINI RAGÙ is a well-flavoured, well-seasoned sauce which is at home on chunky macaroni pasta. It's not in any way difficult and it will leave for dead any bottled sauce you'll find on supermarket shelves. It makes more sauce than you need to dress 500 g of pasta, but any remaining sauce can be refrigerated for two days, or it can be frozen. (There should be enough left to dress pasta for four people, or you could layer up a stack of freshly made crêpes with the sauce and parmesan cheese and bake them in the oven for about 15 minutes till crisp — a sort of light and quick lasagne.)

If porcini sauce doesn't appeal, try the BROCCOLI PASTA. When Zia Flavia first explained this Sicilian sauce to me, I thought it sounded an exuberant recipe to say the least: broccoli, anchovies, pinenuts, garlic, sultanas and saffron. Wow! The Sicilians definitely know how to blend disparate ingredients into dishes of intrigue and good taste. Search out the best anchovies in olive oil for this recipe, as they should be soft and mild, not those smelly furry things that frizzle up and get caught in your teeth.

The bay leaf will help sweeten the air as the broccoli cooks (use it when cooking cauliflower too). Control the urge to drain the broccoli too soon — it needs to be so tender that it can be mashed with a fork.

I adore PHEASANT, and prepared this way, flamed in brandy and cooked gently in stock with diced vegetables, it emerges tender and moist. The birds are no more difficult to joint than a chicken, except the bones are much harder (invest in poultry shears or a cleaver).

Flaming alcohol-based drinks drives off the alcohol, leaving the essence of the spirit. The flames gently singe the outside of the food, developing a depth of flavour. The spirit must be hot, or it will not ignite. The mixture will flame if the dish contains fats or sugar, but rarely if other liquids are present.

It should be remembered that the flames can easily be suffocated by blocking off the oxygen. Keep a lid for the dish, or a metal baking sheet at the ready to place on top should the flames become uncontrollably high. In an emergency, do not attempt to move the cooking dish as the fast movement provides more oxygen and the flames may dart around, lighting flammable items in the kitchen.

If you're having the porcini sauce with pasta, it is too much to have mushrooms in this course too. Either omit them from the pheasant dish, or try the alternate main course.

JERUSALEM ARTICHOKES, sliced thin, turn into crisp golden chips when fried in hot oil and have a faintly earthy flavour — quite unusual. Although the season for them is quite short, they can be refrigerated for several weeks, and emerge as fresh as the day they were dug from the earth (well, almost).

To round off this tasty autumnal menu, a dish of slow-cooked SMOTHERED CABBAGE. Don't throw up your hands in horror: it's tempered with garlic, white wine, vinegar and fennel seeds and is aromatic and savoury, and a good accompaniment to the full-flavoured pheasant. In a similar way, the GRILLED RADICCHIO, SPINACH with a squirt of lemon and the STEWED LENTILS enhance the flavour of the GUINEA FOWL.

GUINEA FOWL were domesticated by the Egyptians and their Italian name, *faraona*, translates as 'hen of the Pharaohs'. I created this dish several years ago to complement the Selvapiana Chianti Rufina Riserva 1968 (bottle no 3083!) I had been given by Signor Giuntini at the Selvapiana Estate in Tuscany.

The stuffing enhances the flavour of the meat, which tastes like a cross between chicken and pheasant. I used red wine (a less precious one, of course) in the cooking liquid to give the dish body and to tie it back to the Chianti, and mellowed it out with a little cream, which gives the sauce a lovely texture and sheen.

If you possess a casserole which can go on the element and which is large enough to hold both birds, great. If you don't, brown the birds one at a time in a frypan, transfer to one or two casseroles, deglaze the frypan with the wine and if necessary, divide the liquid between the two casseroles.

If guinea fowl are not available, the recipe works well with pheasant. Choose two small plump pheasants and cook in the manner described. They will be easier to carve into joints as the bones are a bit softer.

Guinea fowl can also be cooked on the spit or roasted, but the wide breast should always be protected with ham or bacon which provides fat and moisture and prevents the meat from drying out. If filling with stuffing, ensure it contains some kind of fatty meat. The meat also responds well to braising and casseroling.

RADICCHIO from Treviso has long tapered leaves (not round in a ball like the other type) with fat white ribs and red tips. If not available, use witloof.

Finely ground polenta forms the basis of DOLCE AMOR an unusual fruity yeasted dessert cake popular around Como. Although it contains brandy, it cries out for a glass of fine Marsala or a honeyed dessert wine as an accompaniment. It's an ideal cake to serve to a crowd (it's a big mamma!), but it will keep a day or two.

Rigatoni with Isanna's Porcini Ragù

Serves 6 (there will be some sauce left over — see Menu Notes)

25 g dried porcini mushrooms
45 ml (3 tablespoons) olive oil
1 medium onion, finely chopped
500 g minced beef
1 teaspoon salt
90 ml dry white wine
600 g canned Italian tomatoes, mashed
3 tablespoons tomato purée
freshly ground black pepper to taste
500 g rigatoni
salt
parmesan cheese for serving

Put the dried mushrooms in a bowl and pour on 1 cup of hot water. Leave to soak for 30 minutes. Remove with a slotted spoon and place in a sieve; reserve liquid. Rinse mushrooms well under running water, shake, then place on a board. Roughly chop them, then transfer to a saucepan.

Line a sieve with muslin or kitchen paper and strain the mushroom liquid. Strain a second time then set aside.

Put the oil and onion in a heavy-based saucepan and cook gently until the onion is lightly golden. Increase the heat and add the minced beef. Break up the meat with a large fork, then when it is no longer pink, add the salt and pour in the wine. Let the wine evaporate, cooking gently for 10 minutes.

Add the mushrooms and ½ cup of the strained mushroom liquor (or ½ cup stock). Add the tomatoes, tomato purée and pepper, bring to a gentle boil then partially cover with a lid and cook for about 1 hour, stirring occasionally.

The ragù should be thick and pulpy and well seasoned. If required, it can be made a day ahead; cover when cool, then refrigerate.

Cook the pasta in plenty of gently boiling, well-salted water until al dente. Drain briefly and turn onto a heated serving dish. Quickly toss through sufficient sauce to coat. Serve immediately with parmesan cheese.

Zia Flavia's Pasta with Broccoli

Serves 6

750 g young broccoli, well trimmed and separated into
florets (trim off most of the stalk)
salt
bay leaf
45 ml (3 tablespoons) extra virgin olive oil
2 onions, finely chopped
2 cloves garlic, crushed
¼ cup pinenuts
1 tablespoon sultanas
2 anchovies in olive oil
¼ teaspoon saffron strands, soaked in 2 tablespoons warm water
400–500 g cellentani (spiral pasta, sometimes called cavatappi or fusilli)

Cook the broccoli in salted water with the bay leaf until very tender. Drain, reserving the cooking water.

Put the oil in a large frypan and add the onions. Cook gently until golden. Add the garlic and cook for two minutes, then add the pinenuts, sultanas and anchovies. Mash the anchovies into the mixture. Roughly chop the broccoli and add with the saffron and 1½ cups of broccoli water.

Bring to the boil, mashing the broccoli, then lower the heat, cover with a lid and cook gently for 30 minutes, adding more cooking water if necessary. The mixture should be like a thick cream.

Cook the pasta in plenty of boiling salted water until al dente. Drain and tip into the frypan with the sauce. Toss gently and serve from the pan. (If you don't have a large enough pan to toss it in, toss the pasta and sauce together in a heated serving bowl.)

Traditionally, parmesan cheese is not served with this dish.

PHEASANT WITH FIELD MUSHROOMS

SERVES 4–6

*1 plump pheasant weighing about 1.2 kg, cut into 8 small joints, backbone
removed (ask your butcher to do this for you)
45 ml (3 tablespoons) olive oil
60 g butter
salt and freshly ground black pepper to taste
3 tablespoons brandy
1 small onion, finely chopped
1 stalk celery, finely chopped
1 tablespoon flour
2 tablespoons coarsely chopped parsley
2 tablespoons chopped thyme
2 sprigs sage leaves
200 ml stock
1 teaspoon arrowroot
250 g fresh field mushrooms, trimmed, wiped clean with a damp
cloth and thickly sliced or quartered
juice of 1 lemon*

Remove any yellow fat and fatty skin from the pheasant. Rinse the joints and pat dry.

Heat two tablespoons of the olive oil in a large heavy-based casserole over a medium-high heat. When it is hot, drop in less than half the butter and when it has melted, put in the pheasant joints. Brown well on all sides, turning with tongs. Sprinkle over half a teaspoon of salt and grind on some black pepper.

Pour the brandy over the pheasant joints, then ignite it carefully with a lit taper or long match. Turn the joints over in the flames, using tongs, until the flames subside.

Add the onion and celery and cook 4–5 minutes until the vegetables start to soften. Stir in the flour, scatter the herbs over (reserve a little parsley for the mushrooms), then pour in the stock. Bring to the boil, cover with a lid then transfer the casserole to an oven preheated to 170°C for 40 minutes, or until tender. Transfer the pheasant joints to a hot serving dish and cover with a lid, plate or aluminium foil.

Scoop off any visible fat from the juices in the casserole then tip juices into a sieve set over a saucepan and press as much as you can of the onion, celery and juices through the sieve, into the saucepan.

Put the saucepan over a medium heat and stir in the arrowroot dissolved in 2 tablespoons of water. Bring to the boil, boil for 1 minute, then turn off the heat. Test for seasoning, cover with a lid, and reheat briefly before pouring over the pheasant joints.

Heat the last tablespoon of oil in a heavy-based frypan over a medium-high heat. When it is hot, drop in the rest of the butter, which should start to sizzle and foam and turn brown round the edges. Tip in the mushrooms and cook very quickly, stirring often, until tender. Sprinkle with salt, pour on the lemon juice, toss and arrange around the pheasant joints. Sprinkle with a little parsley and serve immediately.

FRIED JERUSALEM ARTICHOKE CHIPS

SERVES 4–6

500 g Jerusalem artichokes
vegetable oil
salt

Peel the Jerusalem artichokes and cut into very thin slivers. Put them in a large bowl, cover with cold water and soak for 30 minutes, changing the water twice. Drain and dry thoroughly on a clean tea towel. Bundle up the artichoke slices in the cloth and set aside until ready to fry them (you can prepare them up to 2 hours in advance).

Heat a 2 cm depth of oil in a deep sauté pan over a medium-high heat (or use a regular deep-fryer). When the oil is hot, carefully lower in the artichokes and fry them until a pale biscuit brown; don't overcook or they become bitter. Transfer to a plate lined with crumpled paper, sprinkle with salt, then tip onto a serving plate. Serve hot.

SMOTHERED CABBAGE

SERVES 4–6

½ large savoy cabbage
1 medium onion, finely chopped
100 ml extra virgin olive oil
2 large cloves garlic, crushed
1 teaspoon fennel seeds
½ teaspoon of salt
freshly ground black pepper to taste
1 tablespoon white wine vinegar

Chop off any hard core from the cabbage and discard, then rinse the cabbage well and slice thinly.

Put the onion in a medium saucepan with the olive oil and cook gently until a rich golden colour, stirring occasionally. Add the garlic and cook 1 minute, then add the fennel seeds and the cabbage. Cook until the cabbage has wilted, turning often with tongs, then season with salt and pepper and pour over the vinegar. Cover with a lid and cook very gently for 1 hour, turning often. If the cabbage dries up, add a tablespoon of water.

Serves 6–8

STUFFING
½ cup raisins
1 small onion, finely chopped
1 stick celery, finely diced
225 g bacon, trimmed of rind and finely chopped
knob of butter
170 g (2 generous cups) fresh breadcrumbs
2 tablespoons finely chopped parsley
¼ teaspoon salt
freshly ground black pepper
70 g (about ¾ cup) coarsely chopped walnuts
1 small egg

MAIN INGREDIENTS
2 small guinea fowl, thawed if frozen
30 ml (2 tablespoons) olive oil
knob of butter
¼ teaspoon salt
freshly ground black pepper to taste
225 g bacon
¾ cup full-bodied red wine
¼ cup cream (optional)
1 tablespoon oil (for stuffing balls)

STUFFING

Soak the raisins in half a cup of hot water in a small bowl while preparing the other ingredients. Put the onion, celery and bacon in a saucepan with the butter, cover and cook gently until soft. Remove the lid and leave to cool. Transfer to a mixing bowl and add remaining ingredients. Blend well, add the raisins and soaking liquid then leave to cool completely. The stuffing can be made a day in advance. The birds must not be stuffed with warm stuffing — cool it first.

Remove any matter from the cavities of the birds and rinse well under running water. Dry off with absorbent kitchen paper. Check all feathers and fluff are removed. Trim feet if still attached.

Fill the cavities with the stuffing but don't pack it in tightly as it needs a little room to swell during cooking. There should be enough left over to shape into a dozen small balls. When the birds are stuffed, stitch the wings and thighs close to the carcass and close up the vent (using either a trussing or carpet needle and fine string). This can be done in advance and the birds kept refrigerated until cooking time. Bring the birds to room temperature before cooking.

If you have a large enough casserole, heat it and add the oil then drop in the butter. Brown one bird at a time, all over, on a medium heat, turning with tongs. Repeat with the second bird. When both are browned, sit both birds breast up in the casserole, sprinkle over some salt and grind on some pepper. Loosely drape the bacon over the birds, then pour in the wine. Immediately cover with a lid and put in an oven preheated to 180°C and cook for 1 hour (cooking time is the same if cooking in two casseroles).

If you managed to fit the birds in one casserole, there will be room to cook the stuffing balls in the oven. Heat a small ovenproof dish with a tablespoon of oil, add the stuffing balls and cook about 40 minutes or until crisp and brown, turning once or twice with two spoons.

If there is not going to be room in the oven to fit both the guinea fowl and the stuffing balls, cook the stuffing balls in advance, before the guinea fowl go in, then reheat in the lower part of the oven.

When the birds are cooked, remove them from the oven and let them rest, covered, for 5 minutes. Transfer them to a board and let the casserole sit tilted a minute or two, then scoop off any fat. Put the casserole on a high heat, add the wine and bubble up to reduce. Add cream if using, taste for seasoning, bubble up again until syrupy, then cover with a lid and turn off the heat.

Cut the guinea fowl into joints in the same way you cut up a small chicken (two thigh joints, two wing joints with a little breast attached and the breast in two). Scoop out the stuffing and transfer the joints of guinea fowl and stuffing to a heated serving platter. Spoon over the hot sauce and serve immediately, accompanied by the stuffing balls.

GRILLED RADICCHIO

SERVES 6

1 kg radicchio di Treviso, or use witloof
extra virgin olive oil
salt
freshly ground black pepper to taste

Trim the radicchio and cut into quarters lengthwise. If using witloof, trim and cut in two down the length. Rub the vegetables with olive oil. Heat a ridged grill pan over a medium high heat until very hot. Cook the radicchio or witloof for a few minutes on each side. Remove from the heat and let rest, covered, for a minute. Transfer to a serving plate, season with salt and pepper and serve hot.

Serves 6

12 small plants of spinach (if large, slice in half through the
root and separate the leaves)
salt
juice of half a lemon
1 tablespoon extra virgin olive oil
freshly ground black pepper

Wash spinach very well, leaving the root end intact (trim if necessary). Bring a large saucepan of water to the boil then add 1 teaspoon of salt. Lower in two or three bunches of spinach at a time, with tongs, holding the stalk end in the water for a minute, then let the leaves flop in as they soften. Total time in the water should be about 1½ minutes.

Lift out with the tongs and plunge into a bowl of cold water. Leave in the water while cooking the next bunches of spinach then transfer to a rack to drain. Repeat until all the spinach is prepared.

Line a rack with absorbent kitchen paper, put a tray underneath, then twirl the bunches of spinach into tiny rounds, gently squeezing out as much water as possible.

Cover with plastic wrap and leave until required (refrigerate if preparing more than 4 hours before required, but bring to room temperature before serving time),

In an electric steamer or a large pan and steaming basket, lined with aluminium foil, place the spinach twirls close together, and cover with a lid. Steam until the spinach is heated through. Press lightly then drain off water. Arrange on a heated serving plate and drizzle with the previously mixed lemon juice, olive oil, black pepper and a few pinches of salt. Serve immediately.

Stewed Lentils

Serves 6

30 ml (2 tablespoons) extra virgin olive oil
1 small onion, finely chopped
½ teaspoon salt
1 bay leaf

1 clove garlic, crushed
freshly ground black pepper
250 g puy (French) lentils, or brown lentils

Put the olive oil in a saucepan with the onion and garlic. Cover with a lid and cook gently for 5 minutes, or until soft. Stir in the lentils, add the bay leaf and pour in 1½ cups of water.

Slowly bring to the boil, turn the heat to low and cook gently about 30 minutes, or until tender, adding a little more water if and when necessary. (The liquid should have evaporated by the end of the cooking: remove lid and reduce if too moist.)
Season with salt and pepper.

1 cup glacé apricots, chopped
200 g plump raisins (such as Lexia raisins)
30 ml (2 tablespoons) brandy
50 ml lemon juice
100 ml freshly squeezed orange juice
4 level teaspoons dried yeast
300 g flour with a few pinches salt
300 g fine polenta or cornmeal
150 g castor sugar
2 sweet apples
30 ml (2 tablespoons) light olive oil
50 g butter
beaten egg for glazing
icing sugar for dusting over the top

Put the glacé apricots and raisins in a bowl and pour on the brandy, lemon juice and orange juice. Leave to soften for 30 minutes. Put the yeast in a bowl and pour on 3 tablespoons of warm water. Leave about 10 minutes, stir, then leave until foamy.

Put the flour, salt, polenta and castor sugar into the bowl of an electric cake mixer. Using the dough hook, briefly blend the ingredients. Peel, core and chop the apples and add to the raisin mixture. Tip into the dry ingredients. Add 200 ml water to the yeast mixture and tip into the mixer bowl. Add the oil and melted butter. Turn on the machine and mix 5 minutes, scraping down the sides of the bowl from time to time.

Brush a 23 cm diameter cake tin with melted butter and sprinkle in a little polenta. Shake it around, then tap out the excess. Pour in the cake mixture, then leave the cake to rise for 2 hours in a warm spot (the cake should fill the tin by about two thirds, and be left to rise to the top).

Brush the surface of the cake with beaten egg, then bake it in an oven preheated to 190°C for about 90 minutes, or until a skewer inserted in the centre comes out clean.

Remove from the oven, loosen the cake from the sides of the tin with a palette knife, then leave it to settle for 10 minutes. Invert onto a cooling rack, turn right side up and leave until completely cold. Dust the top with icing sugar and serve cut in slim wedges.

STREET FOOD COMES HOME

PIZZA

Young, alone and conspicuously foreign — that's how I was when the Italian ship I was travelling on docked in the bay of Naples for a day before finishing its six weeks' journey in Genova. Most of the crew abandoned their shipboard lovers and disappeared into thin air as they fled ashore into the arms of their waiting wives and girlfriends. Older women passengers wept as they realised their attentive companions of the last six weeks were married and that there was no future for them as an officer's wife. Oh, I was so glad to be young and not quite so foolish, and to be taken out for a 'real' Italian meal on land by a gorgeous unattached Italian male. Drinking proper red wine after suffering the 'wine' on board (made from reconstituted powdered dregs) was a treat in itself, but the taste of a sweet rich red tomato sauce on spaghetti sent me into raptures. After landing in Genova I decided to return to Naples for a closer inspection.

And there I discovered pizza. Glorious, crust-popping pizza, cut off in slabs and wrapped in butcher's paper to eat in the streets. Pizzas with thin crusts mottled with charred spots from the wood-fired oven. Pizzas alive with rivers of molten cheese and sweet tomato. Impossible to resist — impossible to exactly replicate at home. I've always loved the smell of food cooking over an open fire — that mixture of smoke and crisping food sends me wild. I'm not tempted by pizza unless I am tantalised by that smell.

PANE AND PIZZA

South of Battipaglia is the ancient city of Paestum, one of the most important archaeological sites in the world. It's worth going out of the way to see. We arrived there late one afternoon, exhausted after a long drive, to find little choice in accommodation. Even worse was the lack of restaurants. We booked into a crumbling grotty hotel, the only place on offer. As soon as we had dumped our bags we fled into the fresh air, escaping the musty smells in the hotel. Our best bet for food was a little *paninotecca* (casual eating and drinking place) called La Casa Vecchia, just across the road from the hotel. It was the wood fire that drew us in; as soon as we got a whiff of the smoke, we decided it was worth a go.

It was peculiar to find ourselves alone in the bar, then alone in the restaurant, and we started worrying that everyone else knew something we didn't. But it was too late to walk out; or rather, too difficult. Peppino (as we christened La Vecchia's proprietor–chef) had us firmly in his grip, ensconced at a chunky table outdoors, and he looked delighted to have company. Then things started happening. Without our ordering them, Peppino delivered a plate of plump black olives. We demolished them in a flash, and flicked their stones into the wood fire, which was roaring away like a furnace. We ordered a carafe of house red, but it tasted like paint stripper, so on special request Peppino produced his 'best' bottle for us, which was, thankfully, just drinkable.

Remo and I watched as he started toasting chunks of country bread over the embers in the front of the fire. A heady whiff of garlic and smoke was a conversation-stopper, and I wished I'd ordered some of whatever it was. I figured other diners must be joining us. Peppino removed the toasted bread to a side plate, the smell of which now had us drooling, and waltzed over to us. It was for us! Good on Peppino: he read us well. He had stuffed a whole clove of garlic in each slice of bread, toasted it on one side over the charcoal embers, then doused the bread with thick golden-green olive oil. Next he sprinkled over oregano and salt. Simple and superb — the best garlic bread we've ever eaten.

Peppino was obviously out for compliments because he excelled himself with the next two courses. *Penne all'arrabbiata* followed. Penne are slim tubes of pasta cut on the diagonal, which allow plenty of rich sauce to seep inside them. The sauce was wonderfully sweet, given a kick with a little chilli and made with the small vine-ripened tomatoes you see drying in doorways of buildings all through the region of Campania. They smell and taste of summer.

While we ate we watched our main course being prepared and cooked, and our spirits rose. Remo chose *capretto* (kid) which was cut into joints and put in a saucepan with oil, then left to roast, uncovered, over the embers. An old lady, Peppino's mother, prodded it and turned it when she saw fit. There ensued a major discussion, which threatened to erupt into an argument, between Peppino and his mother over where to place the pot in the fire, which herbs to use and how long to cook the capretto. The bickering was worth it; the result was succulent and deliciously charred by the wisps of flame and smoke.

I had an excellent pizza — cooked over the fire on a heated slab of stone, kept in the fireplace for the purpose — followed by a salad of dandelion leaves. By the end of the evening we were feeling much more able to cope with our accommodation. Accommodation is more salubrious at Amalfi, on the coast just south of Naples. Amalfi is built right on the cliffs, and in some cases the rock has been dug out by hand to make hollows for houses to fit into. It's an attractive place, with villas hugging the hills around a bay of blue sea. In summer the air is full of the aromas of barbecued seafood and pizzas cooking in wood-fired ovens. With smells as good as this, you know you are in for a good time.

On one visit there, at the tail end of summer, we found an amazing old hotel to stay in. It overlooked the sea, with the

Eggplant Pie

bonus of a free carpark; and the out-of-season rates were reasonable. Our room had an exquisitely patterned marble floor, art deco lamps and French doors with shutters opening onto a little balcony overlooking the hustle and bustle below, and the sea. It was wonderful. We were in love! It was hard not to be.

The main square of Amalfi is set around a magnificent church. Lots of streets lead off the square and we were soon to discover the town was like a rabbit warren. Just when you thought you had it sussed, you got lost, and when you had given up all hope of finding your way home, you'd end up in the square again. We had great fun playing hide and seek.

To choose a restaurant for dinner in Amalfi, all we did was follow our noses. The aromas given off from the pizzas cooking in the wood-fired ovens were tantalising — you simply entered the best-smelling restaurant! The pizzas were crisp and crunchy around the edges; and we ordered them with toppings of bubbling tomato, melting cheese, wrinkly olives, fanned artichokes and prickly anchovies.

Positano is another town well worth visiting outside the main tourist season. The journey between Amalfi and Positano is over winding narrow roads, and is at times perilous. It's a tight fit and car drivers are forced to pull over often to let trucks and buses pass (be prepared to have the paint on the sides of your car scraped); but it's the only route.

Two Exceptionally Bad Meals and Some Atrocious Accommodation

I've written stories mainly of good food; but Italy, like any other food Mecca, has its fair share of shoddy restaurants and dire accommodation, some of which we experienced. In each case we should have known better . . . well, we did know better, but worn down by tiredness or our circumstances, we relented — and later regretted it.

Our first experience was just outside the gates of Pompeii. It was a hot day. The tourists were more annoying than flies as they buzzed back and forth, crawling over each other to peer into yet another ruin. I tried to shut out the commotion, and drifted into another space, another time, as I imagined the Pompeii of old. I was jerked back to reality as I slid on an ancient glazed stone and sprained my ankle. The heat, the dust, the crowds and the pain suddenly became too much and I sat in the ruins of Pompeii and had a good cry. I felt much better afterwards, although I was unable to walk, so we limped off to the nearest watering hole, a touristy hotel directly across from the main entrance to Pompeii.

What a disaster — the food was disgusting. It was so bad, in fact, that we burst out laughing when the waiter slunk up to our table with his watery, overcooked offerings. Was he kidding us? We didn't hang around to find out: we left without eating, and without parting with a lira. An empty stomach was preferable, we commiserated with each other. We decided to drive, to anywhere. We headed towards Sapri on the coast.

Sapri turned out to be a dump, and what's worse, a dump without hotels. It took us an hour, driving around ill-lit streets, to find anything that vaguely resembled accommodation. Eventually we found a hotel, but the less said about it the better. With my leg the size of an elephant's and the atmosphere between us a little frosty after a frustrating day, we decided to fast for a night and catch up on sleep.

The coastline around Sapri offers breathtaking scenery. It's steep and rugged in places, with lots of coves and small beaches with black sand, and that twinkling blue Mediterranean as a backdrop. Marina de Maratea, the first town we came to after leaving Sapri, was brimming with hotels and we kicked ourselves for not travelling the extra few kilometres. Then came Scalea, a big, spread-out town with miles of clean black sand beaches to frolic on. The coastline and surrounding hills are covered in flash villas and hotels, modern places, painted terracotta or dusty pink, with green shutters and potted geraniums. Picture-perfect, laid out for the packaged holiday tourists — not the real Italy.

We drove on through mountains and gorges, expecting ambush at any turn, and eventually halted at a quaint spot on the roadside where we bought fresh bread, rough salami, and beers and had a picnic overlooking the steep cliffs. Then on through towns and villages which seemed to get progressively more depressing. After Pizzo and Vibo Valentia, neither of which tempted us, we went inland and drove through very pleasant countryside dotted with fluffy olive trees, woodsy areas and fields of citrus trees.

Then it turned stormy. It was a real humdinger. The sky was pink and illuminated by forked lightning. Darkness fell rapidly. We drove through the storm, eyes on stalks, looking for an accommodation sign, but nothing turned up. It was amazing to think that a few kilometres back a zillion beds lay empty at Scalea, and here we couldn't find one. After a worrying search, driving through blankets of rain, just before Palmi, in Gioa Tauro, we found a rundown hovel with a dimly lit sign reading *albergo* (cheap hotel). We pulled up and surveyed the scene. It was 7.00 pm, cold, wet, and lightning was flashing all around. We decided to tempt fate and stay in the albergo. We walked into a smoke-filled room to find a few harmless-looking codgers sitting around a table playing cards. They seemed friendly enough, although we obviously puzzled them. Their faces said it all: Who were we, and what were we doing driving through the dark night? We wondered ourselves.

As we went up to our room they clustered around the table, poring over our passports. Obviously, not too many tourists called in. The albergo was deserted, but we were shown to a poky room on the third floor which we were sure was full of fleas. Neither of us fancied getting back in the car to go in search of food, so we resigned ourselves to eating in the albergo. We ordered a house wine, but it was totally undrinkable: so acid and chalky I felt as if my mouth had been vacuumed with a suction pump, then mercilessly sprayed with acid. We ordered a couple of beers. There was no menu, so I suggested something I thought they could handle — a frittata — and prayed it would be made with fresh eggs. God must have been out because my prayer wasn't answered. The frittata was greasy and heavy and sank in my stomach like a stone. Remo was no luckier. He had some greasy grey sausage things which he chased around on the plate and pronounced 'not fit for a dog'. We watched a bit of television with the codgers, then crawled into our pits (narrow single beds). There was not much sleep. The next day we were up at the crack of dawn and out the door as fast as we could go. The storm had died down and left destruction in its path. After Palmi the countryside took a dramatic turn again, with more salubrious accommodation on offer.

There is no lesson to be learned from not booking accommodation in Italy. Often it works in one's favour, allowing more flexibility and enabling you to choose the most attractive place on offer; but sometimes it works against you, when you arrive at night in ill-lit towns with hard-to-find hotels or rundown hovels. Well then, roll out the pizzas and dream of Italy!

STREET FOOD COMES HOME

Erbazzone
Pizza Dough
Garlic Pizza
Pizza Mediterranean
Pesto Pizza
Pizza Bianco
Roasted Shallot and Ham Pizza
Eggplant Pie

My favourite toppings — a combination of Garlic Pizza and Pizza Mediterranean

In a domestic oven it's hard to recreate a typical Neapolitan pizza, with its puffed, thin, crisp crust, mottled with lightly charred spots and tasting faintly of smoke. But invest in a pizza stone and you'll come very close to the real thing, and certainly make pizzas that will leave most commercially prepared products for dead.

First, get your stone — a round or square ceramic slab, fired at a very high temperature. Wash the stone in water (never use detergent) and pat it dry. Heat the pizza stone for about 45 minutes in an oven preheated to 250°C. (The pizza stone must be very hot, so it is a waste of energy to heat it for one pizza only — plan to make several at a time.) Cooking on the hot stone gives a blast of immediate and sustained heat from beneath to ensure the crust cooks at the same time as the topping. It also encourages the dough to puff and bubble, giving some of the authentic look and taste of pizza cooked in a wood-fired oven. Instead of a pizza stone, you can use a new, clean terracotta tile, or bricks. Bricks need to be heated for a little longer, as they are much thicker.

One batch of pizza dough will make one large pizza, enough for two or three people, or two smaller, thinner pizzas. The dough doubles easily, making two large pizzas or four smaller ones. When I make pizza dough, I add gluten to strengthen it.

It is essential to use semolina or cornmeal to prevent the dough sticking when rolling it out. Plain flour goes moist and tacky, and it'll be impossible to get the finished pizza off the work surface and into the oven in one piece. Semolina flour, which is used for fresh pasta, is perfect, but a coarse cornmeal will do. Press or roll the dough into shape on a metal baking sheet, keeping the base well sprinkled with semolina to prevent sticking.

If you are making two pizzas they can be assembled at the same time, but they should be cooked separately, the second one going in the oven as soon as the first is done.

When it comes to a tomato product on top of pizza, you can't beat *passata di pomodoro*, or pre-sieved tomatoes. The passata is not as thick as a purée, which would easily burn, and not watery like some tomato products. It has a good flavour and is seedless.

The toppings suggested in the recipes are mainly barbecued vegetables, whose slightly smoky quality adds a charred flavour, not unlike the taste of pizza cooked in a wood-burning oven. But it's good to experiment with topping ingredients. Salami, ham, smoked chicken and spicy sausage can all be used, along with tapenade and other types of pesto, barbecued or roasted red onions, sundried or semi-dried tomatoes, mushrooms and artichokes . . . the list is endless.

Keep the topping in from the edge, particularly oil or fat-based ingredients such as pesto and mozzarella, because if these bubble over the pizza onto the stone, they impregnate it, burn, and become toxic with successive heating of the pizza stone. Keep any instructions which come with the pizza stone and treat the burns according to the cleaning instructions. Bake the pizzas for about 10 minutes at 225°C. The crust should be crisp and the base lightly browned underneath but tender. Leftover pizza reheats very well in a hot oven. You can also reheat it in a microwave, but the base will not be as crisp.

PIZZA MEDITERRANEAN is my favourite, but the GARLIC PIZZA is the most basic and a good one to start on. The sweet taste of caramelised shallots and ham, accented with the musky potency of marjoram, makes a combination which will appeal to those with a sweeter tooth. The word *bianco* is used not to indicate that PIZZA BIANCO has a white topping, but to show that it is made without tomato sauce. The topping is an unusual combination of asparagus, fennel, garlic and sage leaves. You could substitute well-drained artichoke hearts or bottoms preserved in oil for fennel. PESTO PIZZA is a good way of using up the leftover pesto and the last of the zucchini crop.

Pizza gives a long outdoor lunch a new dimension. Everyone guzzles and gossips, but instead of you cooking for them, they cook for themselves! For a group of ten, you'll need four to five large pizzas. Spread the dough out on the table, surround it with ingredients and let them go for it. The recipes are a guide — you'll find your guests will assemble their pizzas with their favourite ingredients.

Now, something about the other two pies.

Whenever I stay in Reggio Emilia, Isanna and I head off into town at every opportunity to windowshop. It's our little tradition. She wraps her arm through mine and marches me around the shops until we are both exhausted. We cover most of the central shopping area by foot in the morning, pausing now and then to dream about owning some of the exquisite merchandise, or to try on, buy or reject an endless choice of clothes, shoes and handbags. Boy, do we need sustenance to keep us going.

While we duck into a bar for a slurp of water and shot of caffeine (passport to being able to use the toilet), and while I fret about how much I've spent, and how much I know I'm going to spend, she orders slabs of ERBAZZONE, a spinach tart par excellence. There's no time for such serious shoppers to hang around the bar. The erbazzone is handed to us in folded pieces of brown paper, a persistent arm worms its way through mine again, and with handbags and parcels bobbing around our thighs, we walk over the cobbled streets much more slowly now, as we bite into the savoury pastries. Salt licks our lips, flakes of pastry fall to our breasts and remain there. We talk, we laugh, we eat, then we look at each other and communicate our judgement of the erbazzone by eye. Was it as good as yesterday's? Is Mario's better? Is it the best we've had this week?

The only way you'll know if my version is any good is to make it and judge it for yourself. If you happen to be in Reggio, of course, don't fail to grab a slab of it from a bar somewhere. It's wonderful with a crisp sparkling wine, cut into pieces and served as a nibble with drinks, or in larger wedges served with a salad as a light meal.

Curious about the use of corn oil in place of olive oil? It's used in many instances in this region, particularly when a strong olive flavour is not wanted, or when butter is also used in the recipe.

Unlike erbazzone, which can be whizzed up quickly using commercially prepared pastry, the EGGPLANT PIE requires more planning and takes longer to make . But, oh, what a pie! This is knock-their-socks-off stuff. It's a deep pie — make it in a cake tin — filled with rich layers of moist eggplant and tomato with melting globs of mozzarella, all encased in a crisp, flaky pastry case. It's worth the trouble.

If you're pushed for time, use commercially prepared pastry. The dry-baking method used to cook the eggplant is an excellent idea because it uses a lot less oil which cuts down on richness and calories. You need to watch the tomato sauce as it reduces down, stirring it often to ensure it doesn't stick. Pour the eggs in slowly, or they will flow over the top and down the sides, instead of into the pie.

I like this pie served warm, with a tasty collection of salad leaves and black olives, as an outdoor or picnic meal. Although pastry is best eaten the day it is cooked, the leftovers ain't too bad.

ERBAZZONE

SERVES 6–8

1½ cups cooked, chopped spinach
(use frozen cooked spinach, or 2–3 large bunches fresh spinach, cooked)
corn oil
2 tablespoons butter
1 large onion, finely chopped
1 clove garlic, crushed
2 sheets pre-rolled puff pastry, rolled out a little thinner
1 egg
salt
1½ cups freshly grated parmesan cheese
¾ cup fresh white breadcrumbs

Using your hands, wring out excess moisture from the spinach then chop it finely. Heat 1 tablespoon of oil in a frypan over a medium heat. Drop in the butter and while it is sizzling, add the onion. Cook until lightly golden. Add garlic, cook a minute or two, then stir in the spinach. Blend well then take off the heat and leave to cool.

Join the 2 pastry sheets together on an oiled baking tray (dampen the ends with a little cold water to help them stick). Allow excess pastry to hang over the sides of the tray.

Mix the egg, ½ teaspoon salt, cheese and breadcrumbs into the cool spinach mixture. If the mixture seems too moist (plops easily off the spoon), add a bit more cheese and breadcrumbs. Spread over the middle of the pastry, leaving enough room at both ends to fold over and enclose the filling. Bring the ends in to meet the centre and seal them by dampening the edge with a little cold water. Trim to neaten the edges, but ensure the pie is completely sealed. Brush the top lightly with oil, sprinkle generously with salt then prick lightly with a fork. Place in an oven preheated to 210°C and bake for 30 minutes, popping any air bubbles that form during baking with a fork. Serve the pie cut in slices, either hot or warm.

Erbazzone

Pizza Dough

1 teaspoon dried yeast and ½ cup warm water
1 tablespoon olive oil
200 g high grade flour or bread flour
1 teaspoon salt
2 teaspoons gluten (if using bread flour, omit the gluten)
coarse cornmeal

Put the dried yeast in a small bowl and pour in the warm water. Stir once, then leave for 10 minutes until dissolved. Mix in the oil, stirring well. Sieve the flour, salt and gluten into a bowl. Make a well in the centre and pour in the yeast mixture.

Mix together with a large fork, then knead together with your fingers. Turn the dough onto a work surface and knead until smooth. Knead for 8–10 minutes, using a little extra flour to prevent sticking if necessary. Alternatively, knead the dough in an electric food mixer for several minutes with a dough hook, according to the manufacturer's instructions. Put the ball of dough into an oiled bowl, turn it over to coat it in oil, then cover with a damp cloth. Leave in a warm place for 1–1½ hours, or until it has doubled in bulk.

Turn the dough onto a baking sheet sprinkled with coarse cornmeal. Press or roll it into a round circle approximately 32 cm in diameter. Rest the dough uncovered for 5 minutes (or wrap and refrigerate it for up to 12 hours, bringing it back to room temperature before continuing), then assemble the topping as per the chosen recipe.

Meanwhile, heat the pizza stone for about 45 minutes on the bottom shelf of an oven preheated to 250°C then lower to 225°C. Using thick oven gloves, remove the hot stone from the oven to the stove top. Quickly slide the pizza onto the stone, then return it to the oven. Alternatively, use a pizza paddle (a long-handled implement specially designed for the job). Cook the pizza for about 10 minutes, or until it is golden and bubbling on top and browned on the edges. Transfer the pizza to a large plate and serve. If you don't have a pizza cutter (a sharp wheel), use kitchen scissors to snip the pizza into wedges.

Garlic Pizza

½ cup passata di pomodoro, or homemade or ready-prepared tomato sauce
20 small basil leaves
6 balls (150 g) bocconcini mozzarella, drained and sliced
12 garlic cloves, cut lengthwise into quarters
salt and freshly ground black pepper to taste
¼ cup freshly grated parmesan cheese
extra virgin olive oil

Smear dollops of passata or sauce over the pizza dough, then scatter over the basil leaves.

Arrange the mozzarella on top, then the garlic slivers, sprinkle with a little salt and grind on some pepper. Sprinkle over the parmesan and drizzle with oil. Bake as described above.

PIZZA MEDITERRANEAN

1 large eggplant, sliced
olive oil
1 small yellow capsicum, cored, deseeded and cut into small chunks
1 small red capsicum, cored, deseeded and cut into small chunks
½ cup passata di pomodoro, or homemade or ready-prepared tomato sauce
20 fresh basil leaves
6 balls (150 g) bocconcini mozzarella, drained and sliced
salt & freshly ground black pepper to taste
extra virgin olive oil

Brush the eggplant slices with olive oil and bake them on an oiled baking sheet for about 20 minutes, or until a rich golden colour, in an oven preheated to 225°C. The eggplant can be prepared ahead. Alternatively, cook the eggplant on the barbecue.

Put the chunks of capsicum in a bowl and anoint with a little olive oil. Cook them on a hot barbecue plate or rack for about 10 minutes, or until lightly charred. Alternatively, fry them in hot oil until lightly browned and half-tender.

Smear dollops of passata or sauce on the pizza. Arrange the eggplant slices (halved if large), capsicum and basil on top of the sauce, then the mozzarella. Sprinkle with salt, grind on some black pepper, drizzle with oil and bake as described.

PESTO PIZZA

2 slim yellow zucchini
2 slim green zucchini
extra virgin olive oil
¼–½ cup pesto
6 balls (150 g) bocconcini mozzarella, drained and sliced
salt and freshly ground black pepper to taste
12 black olives

If yellow zucchini are not available, use four green ones instead. Slice the zucchini lengthways into long pieces about ½ cm thick. Put the zucchini in a bowl and anoint them with a little oil. Cook them on a hot barbecue plate or rack for about 10 minutes, or until they are lightly charred. Alternatively, fry them in hot oil in a pan until they're lightly browned.

Smear dollops of pesto over the pizza dough, then arrange the zucchini on top. Put on the mozzarella slices, sprinkle lightly with salt and grind on some black pepper. Stud with olives, drizzle with oil and bake as described above.

Pizza Bianco

12 thin asparagus spears
salt
2 fennel bulbs
extra virgin olive oil
fresh sage leaves
6 balls (150 g) bocconcini mozzarella, drained and sliced
8 large cloves garlic, cut lengthwise into slivers
freshly ground black pepper to taste

Trim the asparagus spears and plunge into a saucepan of salted boiling water. Cook uncovered for 4–7 minutes, depending on the thickness. Drain and refresh with cold water, then pat dry (the asparagus can be prepared ahead).

Prepare the fennel by trimming the root end and discarding the stems and any bruised parts. If the bulbs are slim, cut into quarters; if squat, cut into eighths. Place in a bowl, drizzle with olive oil, then cook on a hot barbecue plate or rack for about 10 minutes, or until lightly charred. Alternatively, fry over a moderate heat in a little oil in a frying pan.

Arrange the fennel and asparagus on the pizza dough and dot with sage leaves. Put the mozzarella on top, then scatter on the garlic cloves. Sprinkle lightly with salt, grind on some black pepper and drizzle with olive oil. Bake as described above.

Roasted Shallot and Ham Pizza

12 long-stemmed shallots, trimmed, washed and peeled and split into
bulbs if necessary (or if unavailable, 12 spring onions)
extra virgin olive oil
250 g ham
6 balls (150 g) bocconcini mozzarella, drained and sliced
salt and freshly ground black pepper to taste
1 teaspoon chopped marjoram (or ½ tablespoon dried marjoram)

Put the shallots in a bowl and anoint with a little oil. Either cook them on a hot barbecue plate for about 10 minutes until lightly browned (don't worry if the greenery chars), or fry them in hot oil in a pan until lightly browned. Arrange the shallots and ham on the pizza dough, add the mozzarella, sprinkle with salt, grind on some pepper, scatter over the marjoram and drizzle with oil. Bake as described above.

EGGPLANT PIE

SERVES 8

225 g homemade rich shortcrust pastry flavoured with 1 teaspoon chopped
thyme (or ½ teaspoon dried thyme) and 12 black olives, stoned and chopped
750 g eggplant
olive oil
1 medium onion, finely chopped
2 cloves garlic, crushed
2 x 400 g cans Italian tomatoes, deseeded and diced
2 tablespoons tomato concentrate
salt
1 teaspoon sugar
200 g bocconcini mozzarella, drained and sliced
½ cup breadcrumbs
1 cup freshly grated parmesan cheese
2 eggs

Make pastry in the normal way, adding thyme and olives to dry ingredients after rubbing in the butter. Line into a deep 23 cm loose-bottomed cake tin, reserving a little pastry for a lattice. Prick the bottom and sides of the pastry with a fork, then line with a double thickness of crumpled tissue paper. Fill with baking beans or rice and bake blind 10 minutes in an oven preheated to 190°C. Remove baking beans and paper and bake 10 minutes more, or till the bottom of the pastry is dry.

Slice the eggplant. Brush the slices with oil and lay them on an oiled baking sheet. Bake 20 minutes, or till golden, in an oven preheated to 225°C.

Heat 1 tablespoon of oil in a heavy-based pan, add the onion, garlic and 2 tablespoons of water. Cover and cook till soft. Add the tomatoes, tomato concentrate, ½ teaspoon salt and the sugar. Bring to the boil then simmer, partially covered, for 30 minutes. Remove the lid and cook 30–40 minutes, stirring often, or till thickish and pulpy.

Put a layer of eggplant then a layer of mozzarella on the pastry bottom. Sprinkle with salt, then put in a layer of tomato sauce, breadcrumbs and parmesan. Repeat the layer. Beat the eggs then pour into the tart, making funnel holes with a skewer and encouraging egg to seep in. Reserve a teaspoonful of the beaten egg.

Roll out the scraps of pastry and cut into thin strips. Make a lattice top, using a dab of water to stick the pastry strips onto the rim of pastry. Brush the lattice with egg then bake the pie 40–50 minutes, or till golden brown, in an oven preheated to 190°C. Cool in the tin 10 minutes, lift off the ring and slide the pie onto a serving plate. Serve hottish.

Like any family, the Biuso family has its strengths and its weaknesses, its passions and its pains. The family has grown and changed since I first encountered it in my travels in 1976. Zio Pasqualino, Mamma Rosa's brother who lived with the family for years in Genova (usual story — he came for a week and stayed the rest of his life!), Alfredo, Margot's partner for many years, and Mamma Rosa and Papà Michele are no longer with us. But time can't dim memories.

When I look at Margot's children, Eugenio and Annamaria, I still see them as those two innocent young children with wide eyes and soft milky skin in the vineyard all those years ago — even though Eugenio is now over six feet tall, and Annamaria has grown, matured, and married a handsome man, Giorgio, and borne children. Eugenio is carving out a career in photography, and often travels for his work with his companion of many years, the lovely Aline. It's not difficult to guess Aline's career. She is tall, slim and strong; her dark, glossy hair falls down to her buttocks. She walks confidently, fluidly, and with grace. She's a contemporary dancer, and performs throughout Europe. Ilaria idolises her.

Isanna and Ferruccio's children, Corrado and Valeria, are young adults. Corrado is putting his English to good use in a banking career, and Valeria is a violinist. Their lives are rich and full. Who knows what the future holds for them, and for Annamaria and Giorgio's children Verdiana and Giordano, and for Luca and Ilaria?

Marcella and Alberto, the first of Remo's family to venture to New Zealand, now find themselves in very different circumstances from when we met. Alberto's parents Lisa and Angelo have passed away. Did I ever tell you about them? Etruscan to the bone, Lisa was as thin as a reed and tiny too; and Angelo was a great towering bear of a man — chalk and cheese. Fabulous people. They'd give you their last crumb. Their home was always overflowing with family, but above all the cacophony you'd hear Angelo's husky roar. It was a black day indeed when he passed to the other side.

It fell to Alberto to take up the reins of the Biuso family once Papà Michele took ill. Ferruccio had moved to Reggio Emilia, and Remo had long since flown the nest.

Marcella and Alberto now spend their free time in Querciolo, strengthening bonds with Alberto's Tuscan *famiglia*; and, with Margot, they often dine at Eugenio and Aline's apartment and with Annamaria's new family in Genova.

Miles separate us, but we're a tight-knit family and I know for sure that Mamma Rosa's prayers still echo through all our lives. We get together at every opportunity, but like pieces of a jigsaw, our family picture is only complete when all living members are present.

Our offspring are absorbing the love, the traditions, the culture, the celebration of life focused around the dining table, and are thriving on it. This is our contribution to their well-being — a legacy which we hope will stand them in good stead, and will endure.

WEIGHTS AND MEASURES

Where possible I have put the gram weight of an ingredient and also its measurement in cups, or a physical count of it. This will help those cooks who don't have scales, but it should be remembered that in baking in particular, scales give a more reliable measurement. Cup measures, depending on whether you pack things in, or loosely fill them can vary.

In New Zealand, the USA and in England it should be noted that 1 tablespoon equals 15 ml, but in Australia, 1 tablespoon equals 20 ml. Where this is important, for instance in measurements of oil and vinegar the measurements are in mls first, then in tablespoons, so Australian readers should follow the first measurement (mls) to achieve the desired result. Measurements that won't affect the recipe, such as 1 tablespoon of parsley and so on, have not been converted as a little more or less won't tip the balance.

GRAMS TO OUNCES

General			Exact	
30 g	1 oz	1 oz	28.35 g	
60 g	2 oz	2 oz	56.70 g	
90 g	3 oz	3 oz	85.05 g	
120 g	4 oz	4 oz	113.04 g	
150 g	5 oz	5 oz	141.08 g	
180 g	6 oz	6 oz	170.01 g	
210 g	7 oz	7 oz	198.04 g	
230 g	8 oz	8 oz	226.08 g	
260 g	9 oz	9 oz	255.01 g	
290 g	10 oz	10 oz	283.05 g	
320 g	11 oz	11 oz	311.08 g	
350 g	12 oz	12 oz	340.02 g	
380 g	13 oz	13 oz	368.05 g	
410 g	14 oz	14 oz	396.09 g	
440 g	15 oz	15 oz	425.02 g	
470 g	16 oz	16 oz	453.06 g	

ABBREVIATIONS

g	gram	cm	centimetre
kg	kilogram	ml	millilitre
mm	millimetre	°C	degrees celsius

ALTERNATIVE NAMES

cake tin	cake/baking pan
cornflour	cornstarch
eggplant	aubergine
frypan	skillet
grill	broil
icing sugar	confectioner's sugar
king prawns	jumbo shrimps/scampi
capsicum	bell pepper
spring onion	scallion/green onion
zucchini	courgette

Recipes are based on these (International Units) rounded values

LIQUID MEASUREMENTS

25 ml	(28.4 ml) = 1 fl oz	
150 ml	(142 ml) = 5 fl oz	= ¼ pint
275 ml	(284 ml) = 10 fl oz	= ½ pint
425 ml	(426 ml) = 15 fl oz	= ¾ pint
575 ml	(568 ml) = 20 fl oz	= 1 pint

SPOON MEASURES

¼ teaspoon	1.25 ml
½ teaspoon	2.5 ml
1 teaspoon	5 ml
1 tablespoon	15 ml

In NZ, US and UK, 1 tablespoon = 15 ml
In Australia, 1 tablespoon = 20 ml

CM TO APPROX INCHES

0.5 cm	¼"	5 cm	2"
1.25 cm	½"	7.5 cm	3"
2.5 cm	1"	10 cm	4"

CAKE TIN SIZES

15 cm	6"	23 cm	9"
18 cm	7"	25 cm	10"
20 cm	8"		

OVEN TEMPERATURES

Celsius to Fahrenheit

110°C	225°F	very cool
130°C	250°F	
140°C	275°F	cool
150°C	300°F	
170°C	325°F	warm

180°C	350°F	moderate
190°C	375°F	fairly hot
200°C	400°F	
220°C	425°F	hot
230°C	450°F	very hot
240°C	475°F	

al dente Italian cooking term, literally meaning 'to the tooth' (in other words, cooked, but still firm to the bite). Used to describe perfectly cooked pasta.

anchovies Look for plump anchovies sold in glass. Don't fry anchovies in hot oil as they seize and harden and can become bitter. Cook them gently, stirring, until they dissolve into a paste.

antipasto Italian word used to describe a group of foods served as hors d'oeuvres (plural is antipasti), literally meaning, 'before the pasto' (meal), not 'before the pasta'.

balsamic vinegar This superior vinegar, a specialty of Modena, is made using a centuries-old technique. The juice of trebbiano grapes is boiled down to a sweet syrup, then poured into wooden barrels. It is left for at least five years, and in some cases much longer. The resulting vinegar is aromatic, spicy, and sweet–sour to taste. It should be used sparingly. Most of the cheap balsamic vinegars are based on caramel, not grape syrup.

bird's-eye chillies Small, dried hot chilli peppers, the best substitute for the small hot chilli used in Italy.

capers Capers packed in salt have a truer caper flavour than those packed in vinegar or brine. The salt should be white, not yellowing (which is an indication of age). Wash off loose salt before using and soak the capers in several changes of warm water until they lose any excessive salty taste.

ciabatta Slipper-shaped loaf of bread with a holey texture and a chewy, floury crust.

frittata Italian egg dish, like a flattish omelette.

herbs Herbs are used both fresh and dried in Italian cooking. Italian parsley has flat unfurled leaves with a fresh, grassy, just-picked taste and is always used fresh, as is basil and occasionally mint. Rosemary, bay, sage, oregano and marjoram are used fresh or dried.

lampascioni These small bulbs of the muscari plant (grape hyacinth), are similar to tiny onions and grow wild in southern Italy. Their bitter taste is reduced by blanching then they can be roasted or stewed.

linguine Flat 'tongues' of pasta, commonly eaten with seafood sauces.

Marsala Fortified red wine, from Sicily, available sweet or dry. It can be served as an aperitif or as a dessert wine. Used in cooked savoury dishes, it enriches flavours and gives pan juices a syrupy consistency. It also goes well in sweet fruity dishes and can be flamed.

mascarpone A very rich, mild-tasting creamy 'cheese' used in desserts and savoury dishes.

mortadella A specialty sausage from Bologna traditionally made from pure pork. it has a captivating spicy aroma and a mildly savoury flavour. Available in sizes from 500 g through to 100 kg.

mouli-légumes Also known as a mouli, this inexpensive and almost indestructible piece of equipment is the best way to purée fresh tomatoes (because it catches the seeds, cores and skins) and potatoes (it aerates the potato, making it light, fluffy and lump-free). A food processor doesn't do either of these jobs well because it crushes the tomato seeds, making the sauce bitter, and makes a potato purée gluey.

mozzarella Traditionally this cheese was made from buffalo's milk, but it is now usually made from cow's milk. Sold as a fresh cheese, but also available vacuum-packed in whey. Bocconcini are small bite-sized balls of mozzarella.

olives I recommend using firm Italian or Greek black olives in the recipes in this book as they have good flavour and colour, and do not cook down to a mush that can darken sauces. Add them towards the end of cooking. When green olives are called for, choose large, plump green ones.

panettone A dome-shaped cake, with a light texture and buttery taste, studded with peel and raisins. Popular around Christmas-time.

parmesan cheese (Parmigiano-Reggiano) Has an intoxicating aroma and a spicy flavour with an interesting granular texture. Parmesan look-alikes tend to be highly seasoned, soapy, dry, coarse-textured or inferior in some way. Use them as a grating cheese if you must, but not in Italian recipes calling for the real incomparable parmigiano-reggiano.

Parmigiano-Reggiano also melts without running, browns well, isn't greasy and doesn't become rubbery. It is quickly digested (even by infants) and low in calories. Buy it in the piece and treble-wrap it in aluminium foil. Keep it in the door or the coolest part of the fridge. If storing for a long period, change the foil every so often and wipe the rind clean. For long-term storage, wrap as described and freeze. Grate parmesan as required, because it quickly loses its aroma and flavour.

pesto A rich, green oily sauce, made with basil, garlic, pinenuts, olive oil and parmesan and romano cheeses. The best comes from Genova, they say, because the sea air gives the basil particular character.

pinenuts Seeds of the stone pine, pinenuts are small and creamy-coloured with a nutty, creamy taste. Buy in small quantities as they quickly turn rancid.

polenta The Venetians first bought corn (maize) from its native Mexico to Italy several centuries ago. It's usually a rich golden colour, but in the Veneto region they are rather proud of another variety, white in colour with a less strong corn flavour, and a very smooth texture. Today polenta (nearly always ground from corn, but there is a polenta made from buckwheat, a specialty of Treviso) is a staple food in northern Italy, especially in the Veneto and Lombardy regions, where one is likely to see more corn growing than grapes. The Tuscans are fond of it too; they fry it in wedges and serve it under rich game birds, or use it instead of toasted bread under hot antipasti. Polenta is often sold preboiled, in a slab, ready to fry, grill or bake.

porcini mushrooms Earthy, woodsy-smelling richly-flavoured mushrooms (Boletus edulis), available fresh in autumn and spring, and dried, all year round. Drying them intensifies their aroma and taste, and they impart a powerful mushroom flavour to any dish they are added to. Dried porcini are usually sold in small cellophane bags; make sure you choose a bag with large, pale pieces of porcini, not one full of crumbs and dust. Stored airtight, they last for many months.

poussin A baby chicken.

prosciutto This famous ham from Parma (sometimes referred to as Parma ham) is sold either as prosciutto crudo, a raw ham cured by air and salt (not, as is often presumed, by smoking), or prosciutto cotto, a cooked version. In this book prosciutto refers to the raw, cured ham. Prosciutto crudo is sweet and delicate with creamy, sweet-tasting fat. It is sliced very thin and eaten as an antipasto component or used in pasta sauces and stuffings. Substitute thinly sliced ham off the bone if you have to.

radicchio 'Rosso di Verona', a red-leafed vegetable, looks like a small red cabbage. Used raw in salads, it has a pleasantly bitter taste that works well with strongly flavoured dressings made with garlic, capers and mustard. 'Radicchio di Treviso' has long tapering leaves, is less bitter and is best doused in olive oil and grilled, or used in risottos and sauces.

ricotta cheese A soft curd, low-fat cheese made from whey, ricotta is a byproduct of cheesemaking. Used in savoury and sweet dishes.

risotto rice This variety of rice has stubby grains which have the ability to absorb plenty of flavoursome liquid while it giving out a creamy starch, yet is still maintains a firm 'al dente' structure. *Arborio* rice, proably the best known and most freely available variety, makes a sticky risotto, but each grain can still be separated from the mass. *Vialone nano* is particularly good for Venetian-style risottos, where the desired result is a little more liquid than risottos from other regions. Perhaps the best, but hardest to find and the most expensive, is *carnaroli*, which produces a rich creamy risotto while maintaining a firm texture. Do not attempt the risotto recipes in this book with any other types of rice.

Roman or plum tomatoes Egg-shaped tomatoes with plenty of flesh and few seeds, which makes them ideal for sauce-making.

salt The most indispensable ingredient in the Italian kitchen, salt, when used correctly, is the cook's best friends. It draws out those nuances of flavour which, had the food been left unsalted, may have lain dormant. Salt sprinkled on cooked food is not the same; you are likely to taste only salt.

spaghettini A thinner spaghetti, ideally suited to tomato sauces and sauces made with small seafood.

stock Italian stock (*brodo*) is much lighter than French stock. It is usually made from veal bones or chicken carcasses, or both, and vegetables. Use vegetable cooking water or diluted chicken stock as a substitute.

tomato products Tomatoes need plenty of exposure to full sun to develop that wonderfully sweet tomato flavour. In most instances in this book, I have recommended canned italian tomatoes because they are a superior product to the watery, hot-house or hydroponically grown tomatoes usually available out of season.

Passata is a brand name for tomatoes which have been skinned, cored, deseeded and pulped. It is the same type of purée you get if you mash canned Italian tomatoes, minus the seeds. The product is rich and sweet and makes excellent sauces.

trenette Ligurian name for pasta similar to tagliatelle, nearly always served with pesto.

witloof Chicory grown in sand to produce tender white leaves in a tight bud, or chicon — used in Italian cooking since the late 16th century.